Comedia Series ● No 13

MICROCHIPS WITH EVERYTHING
The consequences of information technology
Edited by Paul Sieghart

Comedia Publishing Group
9 Poland Street, London W1V 3DG Tel: 01-439 2059
in conjunction with the
Institute of Contemporary Arts
Nash House, The Mall, London SW1 Tel: 01-930 0493

Comedia Publishing Group was set up to investigate and monitor the media in Britain and abroad today. The aim of the project is to provide basic information, investigate problem areas, and to share the experiences of those working in the field and to encourage debate about the future development of the media. For a list of other Comedia titles see page 151.

First published in 1982 by Comedia Publishing Group
9 Poland Street, London W1V 3DG Tel: 01-439 2059

ISBN 0 906890 32 2 (paperback)
ISBN 0 906890 33 0 (hardback)

Comedia and the Institute of Contemporary Arts gratefully acknowledge the encouragement and assistance of Dewe Rogerson Limited both in the promotion of the July 1982 seminars and in the production of these edited transcripts. In their work as the national advertising and public relations agency for Information Technology Year, Dewe Rogerson Limited always perceived the ultimate value of debating the management of the changes which IT will certainly bring: the company worked with the Institute of Contemporary Arts, among many others, to bring home "ITs Consequences" to a public frequently bemused by the punditry or absorbed by the gadgetry.

Design by Julian Stapleton

Drawings by David Austin—many of these drawings originally appeared in Computer Weekly.

Typeset by Manchester Free Press
Bombay House, 59 Whitworth Street, Manchester M1 3WT (061-228 0976)

Printed in Great Britain by
Unwin Brothers Limited, The Gresham Press, Old Woking, Surrey

Trade distribution by
Marion Boyars, 18 Brewer Street, London W1 Tel: 01-439 7827

Contents

PREFACE

The essays in this volume are based on contributions made at a series of five seminars entitled *IT's Consequences: The Social and Political Implications of Information Technology* organised by the Institute of Contemporary Arts in July 1982. The series set out to be challenging: it was designed to ask questions, not to pre-judge answers. The complexities of the Information Technology debate tend to have been crystallised too simply into pro and anti positions. A polarisation which has been exacerbated both by the predilection of the media for provocative black and white banner headlines, and by the critics and defenders of IT themselves. Rather than pretend that this problem did not exist, the ICA series confronted it head on by bringing together exponents of both 'camps' in the hope that, through discussion, a more positive, thoughtful and complete picture would emerge. During the course of the debates the Home Office shared a platform with the National Council for Civil Liberties, heads of computer companies met with Trades Union leaders etc. No one imagined that they were all going to agree. But they were encouraged to get off their soap boxes and talk together. The role of the audience in this was crucial. The audience listened, challenged, exchanged and sometimes changed ideas. By the same token the most important contributor to this book is the reader. The essays are diverse points of reference. The beginning not the end of discussion.

It may seem curious to some that a series on Information Technology was held at the Institute of Contemporary Arts. It has always been a central concern of the ICA both to initiate debate on contemporary cultural issues and to intervene at critical moments in such debate so that discussion may be had before policy is determined. It is easy to see why technology is the legitimate concern of a cultural institution where that technology has a direct impact on a cultural medium such as television. But where is the connection between a cultural instution and the discussion of work patterns or North/South relations? The fact that this question can be posed, as it was during the course of the debates, demonstrates an interesting dislocation in our notions of culture since the Oxford English Dictionary's 1805 definition of culture as 'the intellectual side of civilisation'. It is this broad definition of culture to which the ICA is proud to adhere.

And a series on technology held at the ICA, rather than at a technical college for instance, becomes a direct challenge to the contemporary myth that technology is somehow 'other' from

human life: that technological progress acts independently of the needs of ordinary people and is necessarily the preserve of a set of 'objective experts'. Whereas, of course, in as far as technology both changes the way we live our lives and affects our perceptions of the world — as witnessed by the Industrial Revolution — it is of essential concern to everyone. It was in this spirit that the ICA series of public debates was conceived. And it is in this spirit that I hope this book will be received.

And, finally, why hold the series in 1982? The answer lies partly in the 'critical moment' philosophy already expressed. But much is also due to the work of the IT82 Committee in their campaign to heighten public awareness of the issues in this government designated Year of Information Technology. And I should like to take this opportunity of thanking the Committee for their imaginative support of the series. Support which demonstrated the broadmindedness of their approach; for they were prepared to take on the fears engendered by Information Technology as well as to laud its benefits. Special mention must also go to Dewe Rogerson for the promotion of the series and financial support of this book.

My grateful thanks are also due to all those who gave advice on the series. Especial thanks to Rory Johnson for his tireless provision of information; to Paul Sieghart for his elegant and efficient work as general editor; and to Charles Landry and Brian Whitaker for their energy and enthusiasm without which this book would never have been published.

Nicky Singer
Associate Director of Seminars
ICA, The Mall, London SW1

IT in our times: or down among the baboons

PAUL SIEGHART

In the UK, the government declared 1982 to be Information Tech-nology Year. As it was willing to back that declaration with some real support in the form of cash and other resources, the Year has in fact stimulated a good deal of interest in the subject. One of its more imaginative events was a series of five summer evening seminars on *IT's Consequences*, organised by the Institute of Contemporary Arts in The Mall, London, on which this book is based.

Each seminar concentrated on a different aspect of IT, which the speakers addressed from their particular points of view. Some spoke from full written texts others from notes. All of them had interesting and important things to say. What we have tried to do in this book is to bring all those contributions together, so that they can reach a wider audience. Each chapter contains the edited papers contributed to one of those evenings, introduced by a brief preface of my own.

I was also invited to contribute a general introduction to the book as a whole, and given a free hand to say whatever I wanted to. Such invitations are irresistible: they give one a unique chance to get all sorts of half-baked (and even quarter-baked) ideas into print. I have watched this whole area of IT — and its consequences — grow and develop over the years; sometimes with excitement; often with frustration; but always with fascination. Here, therefore, is how it seems to me now — deliberately with a broad-brush approach, and no attempt at any academic rigour. If any of that is controversial or provocative, all the better: we are still nowhere near a final answer to any of the problems which IT presents for us, and we can only get nearer by constantly asking new questions.

Chips and experts

First, a few words about the microprocessor, or 'chip', which lies at the centre of the current debate. It is an engaging little object. As it's usually encased in black plastic, you don't normally see it. But even when you do, you need a microscope to appreciate its full beauty. Wafer-thin and no more than about 5 mm square, with a couple of dozen or so very thin wires sticking out from the edges, it contains thousands of minute electrical circuits. All that happens is that, if you send some electrical pulses up some of the wires, other pulses come down some of the others. Nothing could be more harmless in itself. And the chips have many of the modern virtues: they consume virtually no energy; they do not pollute the biosphere; and they do not exhaust any scarce resources − their principal component, silicon, is the main constituent of sand.

But, though the chip develops no physical force, its potential for intellectual performance can be immense. Its primary use is to 'process' or 'handle' information, at tremendous speeds and in a highly sophisticated and reliable fashion.

Its design and operation is extremely complex, and well beyond the understanding of anyone who does not have years of training and expertise in this area. To those who are not already such experts, the best piece of advice I can give is not even to try to understand the technical side. What is important for all of us is *what* chips can do − or, more accurately, what people can make them do − and not *how* the chip does it. The most dangerous cop-out in today's high-technology world is to say'The technology is beyond me, so there's no point in my trying to express any views on how it ought to be used.' There is *every* point: unless people form their own views, and make them known, they will simply be ignored by those who have to take the important decisions. That can be decidedly dangerous. Not because the decision-makers will necessarily set up malign conspiracies to manipulate and control the rest of the population. Few of them do: most of them simply try to do a difficult job, by their own lights, to the best of their abilities. But they can hardly be expected to design their policies to suit other people if they don't even know what it is that those people want.

It cannot be said too often that no one needs to understand any technology in order to form a view on what should or should not be done with it. You don't need to know how aeroplanes are constructed or how they work in order to decide how safe (and therefore how expensive) you think they ought to be. You don't need to know how a medical respirator works in order to decide whether it should be used to prolong the lives of people who can never recover any of their human functions, or of people who want to die. You don't need to know how telephones can be tapped in order to decide whether they should be tapped at all — and, if so, by whom and for what purposes. (For instance, to catch murderers and heroin smugglers only? Or perhaps tax evaders too?) You don't need to know anything about coaxial or optical fibre technology to decide whether or not we should have cable TV; if so, how many channels; whether they should be used for commercial or public service programmes, or for public access communications; and who (if anyone) should have what sort of control over the programme contents. You don't need to understand how numerically-controlled machine tools or robots work in order to decide whether we should be installing more or fewer of them.

And the same goes, the other way up, for the experts. Knowing how chips function — indeed, even designing, programming or using them — is neither a necessary nor a sufficient qualification for forming views on how they ought to be used. You may be better qualified than others to know what they *can* do, but not what they *ought* to do: there is no specialist expertise in morality or politics. In this field, an expert can have a specific and important function as a whistle-blower: he may see a future development on the horizon long before it becomes large enough for others to see. But he has no greater competence than anyone else to say whether that development is a threat, or a promise, or both; let alone what we ought to be doing about it now. For the same reason, the expert in any technology bears no special responsibility for how others use it, and his share of the blame for any abuse is no greater than anyone else's. Atomic weapons are not detonated by scientists, but by politicians and soldiers. And if IT is abused for evil, rather than used for good, that will not be the fault of the IT experts.

What is IT?

Next, IT itself. There is still a good deal of confusion about what this actually *is*. In fact, it is not just one technology, but the combination of two separate ones: computing and telecummunications, both using electrons as the medium for their performance. Apart from the electrons, there is nothing new in either computing or telecommunications. The Chinese, the Koreans and the Japanese have been using the abacus for computing since well before the beginning of the Christian era, and still do: in the Far East, public contests between one star performer on the abacus and another on the electronic calculator are close-run things, and the abacus still sometimes wins by a short head. Likewise with telecommunications: long before writing was invented, people sent each other messages by hill-top bonfires and prairie smoke signals; African village drummers still communicate at the speed of sound (around 700 miles an hour) over great distances; and nearly 200 years ago the British Admiralty could already get a signal from London to Plymouth by semaphore at a speed of around 10,000 miles an hour on a clear day.

The real revolution came through harnessing the electro-magnetic phenomenon — especially in the from of very brief ('digital') pulses — to both these purposes. As such pulses travel at around 186,000 miles a *second* through space or air, and almost as fast down metal wires, both computing and telecommunications have become enormously faster. What is important about this is that a far greater *volume* of them can be performed in a given time. It is not just that it now only takes one millionth of a second to work out that two plus two make four and to communicate that result to some remote

point; but that a million such calculations can now be made and communicated in the second that it used to take to make and communicate just one. And, with the cheap mass production of chips, the costs of such operations are plunging even faster than the speeds are rising.

Nor is all this just confined to information in the form of numbers, letters or other symbols: it applies today to information in *any* form – including of course colour pictures. Instead of seeing a single photograph of the Royal Wedding, the launching of the Space Shuttle, the rape of Beirut or the sinking of HMS Sheffield in the newspaper a day or more after the event, anyone anywhere in today's world can see it, in full colour, as it is actually happening – that is, in 'real time' – provided they have access to the electronic network in which the information is circulating.

What is information?

Curiously, despite the advances in IT and its pervasive influence today, there is still no generally agreed definition of 'information'. Indeed, one of the more prevalent confusions is still that between 'data' and 'information'.

Data is the plural of the Latin noun *datum*, 'that which is given'. So data are the things that are given – the figure 6, say, on Jane Smith's front door, or indeed the names Jane and Smith which she was given at birth. Data by themselves have no meaning: if I broadcast the figure 6 over all the world's communication channels, no one is any the wiser, nor even better informed. But if I say 'Jane Smith lives at No. 6', I am communicating *information*, because that statement can increase the *knowledge* of someone who hears it and did not know it before. Data can only become information when they are combined together in some form which can increase the knowledge of a receiver. The world is full of data, which are meaningless in themselves. Information therefore presupposes the existence of intelligent beings who understand each other: at least one of these beings has to select some data from the orderless muddle in which s/he finds them, and string them together into some order which will have meaning for another intelligent being; that ordered string then constitutes information from which such other beings can increase their knowledge. What they do with that knowledge is yet another question; they may, for example – or again they may not – use it to increase their wisdom.

The transformation from each step to the next involves an operation. Computers, programmed by intelligent beings, can transform data into information; telecommunications, designed by intelligent beings, can communicate information to other intelligent beings who can transform it into their knowledge; once they have that knowledge they can, if they wish, transform it internally into wisdom.

Information as a commodity

So much for the sequence by which information is *produced* from data, and *distributed* to users who *consume* it in order to increase their knowledge and (it may be) their wisdom. All that has a familiar ring: production, distribution and consumption are functions that we know well enough in the context of other goods and services. We might therefore expect information to behave like any other commodity of commerce, subject to the familiar economic laws of supply and demand, the price mechanism, etc. But we would be unwise if we did, for the analogy soon breaks down. Other commodities obey these laws because they are finite, and therefore potentially scarce. There is only so much copper in the world, and the physical law of the conversation of matter ensures that we cannot destroy what there is, or create more of it out of nothing. Supply and demand will therefore balance at the price which someone is willing to pay for an extra ton.

Not so in the case of information. Whatever it may cost me to string it together from its constituent data (and that may be a good deal), once I have done that *it can be multiplied without limit at virtually no extra cost.* In the form of print, the photocopier can reproduce it in thousands of copies. Fed into a broadcast channel, millions can hear it on their radios or see it on their TV screens. Held in a computer store, thousands can retrieve it on their remote terminals.

Perhaps more important still, you cannot deprive me of 'my' information by acquiring it yourself. If you take a photograph of the letter marked 'private and confidential' that you find lying on my desk, you do not deprive me of the letter or of the information in it. So, since the principal characteristic of 'property' is that, by stealing it, you can deprive the lawful owner of its use and enjoyment, *there can be no property in information.* Quite apart from that consideration, the idea of regulating people's rights to information by some concept of ownership doesn't work anyway. Who, for instance, owns my date of birth? Me? My mother? The maternity hospital? The Registrar of Births, Marriages and Deaths?

In short, trying to treat information as if it were a commodity like any other is dangerous and misleading. A string of data, ordered in a particular sequence, has no material existence and can be reproduced without limit. While it is true that, like other commodities, it can be 'produced', 'distributed' and 'consumed', it does

not behave like a commodity in any other way.

Information and power

We are often told that 'information is power'. Strictly, it isn't.
Knowledge, suitably used, can help you to acquire power over your
environment — including the other people who form part of it. So,
information can *lead* to power, but only if it is first transformed into
knowledge, and that knowledge is then appropriately used. Strictly,
therefore, some information may be a *necessary* condition for the
exercise of some powers, but no information can be a *sufficient*
condition for the exercise of any power. Just having access to
information will not by itself give you power.

On the other hand, the converse of that last proposition is
undoubtedly true: if you do *not* have continual access to information, you can neither acquire power over your environment, nor
keep it for long if you already have it. So, depriving people of
information can put them at a severe disadvantage, even to the
point of barring them altogether from some things they want to do.
Without accurate maps, few journeys are likely to end at their
intended destinations. And, once there *are* accurate maps, those
who have them can get to their destinations more quickly, cheaply
and surely than those who have not.

So, in a modern world in which vast quantities of potentially useful information have already been put together, and more is being accumulated every day, there are great economic and other advantages in being able to *control* the flows of such information – that is, in being able to decide who shall have access to it and who shall not. If you want to keep others away from your private Eldorado, make sure they can't get the map which tells them how to reach it – or at least that they can't decipher it if they do get hold of it.

In short, if you can make information scarce, then it *will* behave like a commodity. And, like everything else that flows, information can only flow through *channels* of one kind or another – printing presses, wires, optical fibres, radio frequencies, satellites and the like. Those are always finite – and whoever can control them, or what goes into them, can therefore make information artificially scarce, and so determine the balance of power between many different people and their interests.

Which is why, for as long as people have sought power – whether political or economic – they have sought to exercise control over communication channels, and the information that goes into them. A crude way of doing that is by direct censorship. More subtle ways are the licensing of printing presses or newspapers (as in many modern dictatorships), or the restrictive allocation of paper, typewriters and copying machines (as in Eastern Europe). There is only a limited spectrum of radio frequencies, so there has to be some agreed control over the allotment of channels to would-be broadcasters; but in most countries governmental control over radio and TV goes far beyond what is necessary for that purpose alone. Various branches of the law offer other opportunities: the laws of libel, contempt of court, official secrets, confidentiality, copyright, patents, etc. can all be used to control different information flows.

Needless to say, whenever someone tries to increase his power – for instance, by restricting information flows – others will oppose him. The movement for 'freedom of opinion' and 'freedom of expression' is therefore as old censorship and licensing. At the level of international law, it has now long since won its cause: these freedoms have been formally recognised as universal human rights ever since 1948. But at the level of national and international practice, it still has a long way to go. All over the world, people continue to languish in prisons and camps because of what they have thought, said or written; and in those countries, what the press is allowed to print, or the media to broadcast, bears little resemblance to any objective truth. And very few governments yet regard themselves as being under any obligation to give people ready access to all the official information they need – hence the current movement for 'freedom of information'.

So the extreme and unjust inequalities of power which the control of information flows makes possible remain preserved in far too many places. But by no means all. Even before the most recent developments in IT, modern communications techniques have wrought some crucial changes. The transistor radio has revolutionised life in some parts of the Third World. TV has revolutionised people's understanding of what actually goes on elsewhere. All over the world, attitudes and expectations have changed out of all recognition, in just one generation, through these new information flows. And that whole process is still only in its early stages. With it has come yet another new movement, which calls for an expansion of the existing human rights of freedom of opinion and expression into a new 'human right to communicate', combined with a 'New World Information and Communication Order'.

In the foreseeable future, IT will make *possible* yet more new information flows which have never before been dreamt of, and which could have dramatic effects for either good or evil. My own view is that, like every other technology, IT is morally neutral. In itself, it is neither malign nor benign. Everything will depend on what people do with it: whether they use it for good ends, or abuse it for evil ones. (That is true, by the way, for every technology that has ever been devised: even the humble typewriter was the instrument which communicated Adolf Eichmann's transport orders, and so formed one of the tools for sending millions to their doom.)

So how *will* people in fact use IT? To reinforce and aggravate unjust power structures, so that IT will become yet another tool of oppression, persecution, exploitation and deprivation? Or to promote and support liberty, equality, fraternity, democracy and all the rest of our most exalted ideals?

Two polarised positions

As the Great Chips Debate rolls on, that is the $64,000-question around which all the others cluster. Two opposing positions are now emerging among the general noise. There are the optimists, who see IT as mediating the millenium for mankind; and there are the pessimists, who can only see worse doom and gloom coming out of it all. The optimists foresee abundance, comfort, leisure, creativity and fun; the pessimists warn of unemployment, de-skilling, pervasive social control and surveillance, and increasing inequalities in wealth and power.

This polarisation is familiar: the two positions are very similar to those taken in the Great Nuclear Debate. And that is not the only thing that the two debates have in common. Both are about new technologies, based on branches of science too recondite for most people to understand. Unlike steam engines, mechanical looms and lathes, or even aeroplanes, both atomic energy and IT are opaque and therefore mysterious. They are also immensely powerful: what an atomic bomb can achieve in destruction, or a giant computer system in information processing, is 'astronomical' by comparison with what was familiar before. Mysterious power is both exhilarating and frightening, so it is not surprising that each of these new technologies evokes elation in some, and terror in others. And just as the first we knew of atomic power was Hiroshima, which left the mark of Cain indelibly imprinted on that technology, so the first public perception of the power of IT came through George Orwell's prophetic satire *1984*.

But all that is not enough to explain the whole phenomenon of polarisation and confrontation over these two technologies. On both sides, there are many perfectly rational, intelligent, thoughtful and mature people, not normally given either to wild elation or to abject terror. How do they manage to come to completely opposite conclusions about the same thing? Take the effect of IT on employment, for instance. Suppose, at some far-distant limit, all the goods and services we could possibly want were to flow off automated production lines with virtually no human effort. Why does one side see this as the ultimate achievement of the Land of Milk and Honey, and the other as the purgatory of mass un-employment? Plainly, they cannot both be pursuing the same ideals and lifestyles. And there may lie an important clue, whose pursuit requires a digression into some very speculative territory.

Chips, chimps and baboons

Two of our closer relatives among the higher apes pursue lifestyles which bear striking similarities to some aspects of our own, but in very different ways. The chimpanzees munch their way gently through the rain forest, at a rate of about half a mile a day. There are few predators, and there is always more than enough to eat. The apes associate in loose bands; their social structure, such as it is, is largely egalitarian. They display next to no aggression to each other, or indeed to anyone else. When bands meet, they have a party, and exchange a few members. When a female comes on heat, she copulates with just about every male in sight. There is no sexual guilt, and no sexual possessiveness. Everyone cossets the babies. Everyone grooms everyone else. So far as we can see, the chimp lives a happy, relaxed life of innocence in the Garden of Eden.

Outside the rain forest, in the dry and open savannah, lives the baboon. For his kind, life is nasty, brutish and short. Food is hard to come by. There is nothing like enough vegetable matter, so some smaller animals get killed and eaten. Predatory cats abound, and there is little shelter from them. So the baboon lives and hunts in a tightly organised tribe. The organisation is strictly hierarchical: one dominant male (the 'greyback') at the top, all-powerful until he is eventually overthrown by a palace revolution among the 'barons' just below him, and then a strict pecking order all the way down to the bottom of the social ladder − constantly reinforced by dominance and deference rituals straight out of *Clockwork Orange*. Within such a tribe, loyalty to the group is paramount. When two tribes meet, they fight to the death over their territories. When a female comes on heat, there are apt to be bloody battles over her among the lusty males; the one that wins will not leave her side again until she has ceased to attract. The babies are brought up dead tough. Not a pretty sight, but it works: though the environment is hostile, the baboon survives.

Anyone who has read Jane Goodall's accounts of the lives of these two species, or seen her marvellous films, will have recognised rather too many parallels for our own comfort. So have zoologists like Konrad Lorenz and Desmond Morris, in books like *On Aggression*, *The Naked Ape*, and *The Human Zoo*. In our ideals of liberty, equality, fraternity, the pursuit of happiness, loving our neighbour, peace, democracy and all the rest of them, we aspire to the Paradise of the chimp. In the reality of our daily lives − especially those of corporate, official or military man − we spend much of our time emulating the Purgatory of the baboon. The whole sad tale is encapsulated in the myth of the Fall, which has a close (and probably historical) parallel, at least among the apes: as the rain forests shrank through climatic changes some millions of years ago, the baboons' ancestors were forced out and had to adapt their behaviour to ensure survival in a hostile environment of permanent scarcity and danger: those who managed to stay behind were the progenitors of the modern chimpanzee. Our ancestors, too, scraped a precarious and dangerous living in the savannah for a very long time. Had they not adopted many behaviour patterns like those of the baboon, probably none of us would be here today.

And so, put at its simplest, one might say that the tragedy of the human condition is that we wish we could emulate the delightful chimp, while in fact we seem to be impelled to behave much more like the horrid baboon.

None of this, of course, is rigorously scientific: there are many missing links and untested hypotheses. Nor is it ever legitimate to draw firm inferences for *homo sapiens* from the behaviour of other species. But at the speculative level, it helps to explain at least some things which seem otherwise quite inexplicable.

Such as, for example, some of the irreconcilable positions in the Great Chips Debate, which is where we left that subject. If we could all behave like the lovable and loving chimp, what would we have to fear from an abundance of automatically-produced goods and services? If we need no longer earn our bread by the sweat of our brows, why could we not use our enhanced leisure to lie back and enjoy ourselves, reaching for the nearest microwave-cooked hamburger at the first rumbling in our bellies, or the nearest chip-certified infertile sexual partner at the first stirring a little lower down?

If, of course, we are fated to behave like the unloving and unlovable baboon even in an economy of abundance, life could not be like that. Instead, greed, envy and the lust for power would ensure that the strongest continued to grab the baron's share of whatever was available, even if it was vastly more than they needed, and even if it deprived those at the bottom of the pecking order of their most basic needs. Power, goods and services would continue to be unequally distributed − indeed, more unequally than now, since there would be more to maldistribute, and better techniques for maldistributing it. Man would continue to exploit, oppress, persecute and deprive his own kind, all the more effectively with the use of the new technology.

So which is to be? If, by our own efforts, we can restore the abundance of the rain forest, can we also recover within ourselves the behaviour patterns of the Garden of Eden, or are we saddled forever with the inheritance of a few million years of life in the inhospitable savannah? In short, is our baboonishness now part of our irreversible nature, or is it passed on only by reversible nurture?

Social engineering

The future of every human society depends crucially on the answer to that single question. So does the validity of every attempt at social engineering, which is doubtless why the question is politically so highly charged. To the convinced Marxist, for instance, anything that smacks even remotely of 'sociobiology' is anathema, contrived by the scientific lackeys of international monopoly capitalism in order to keep the toiling masses under its yoke for even longer. It is all a little like race and IQ, but with even less evidence either way. At the other end of the political spectrum, traditional reactionaries remain convinced of the inherent baseness of man, and of the consequent need for authority structures to repress evil-doing, and so to preserve the established order.

More recently, the animal ethologists have come up with an even more worrying idea, well described in Richard Dawkins' *The Selfish Gene*. Take a society composed of a mixture of hawks and doves – the avian equivalents of baboons and chimps. A single pair of hawks could decimate a large population of doves, and so reproduce its own kind at the expense of theirs. But too many hawks will also decimate each other, so there is a survival advantage for them in having quite a lot of doves around. Zero-sum games theory predicts that there will be a point of balance in the proportion of the two kinds which will be stable: that is, an excursion from that point either way will work to the disadvantage of the growing group, and so the proportion will tend to revert again to the original point. That too has a familiar ring in human societies: not only do they tend to oscillate stably between periods in which chimp-like and baboon-like fashions are in the ascendant, but the proportion of successful hawks (heroes, popular leaders, managers, adventurers, bullies, hypocrites, mountebanks and other variants) seem to remain

remarkably constant, throughout the ages and in different civilis-
ations, among a majority of successful doves (subservient and faith-
ful followers, and other helpless, harmless, hapless or feckless
members of the toiling masses).

Must it always be so? Is humankind perfectible, or even just
improveable, by its own planned efforts? Or will those who start off
as idealistic planners always end up as realistic bosses (if their
colleagues have not meanwhile eliminated them in the struggle for
survival), as has happened so often in the past?

So far, we simply do not know enough about ourselves to be able
to make any reliable predictions about any of this. The outlook
from history is not encouraging. Very few human communities have
ever been recorded as surviving for long on a footing of love,
equality and the free sharing of their goods and services: the Tro-
briand Islanders and perhaps a few others in the South Seas before
western adventurers discovered them; some (but not many) Ama-
zonian tribes; perhaps some monastic houses in Europe and Tibet.
The best known was a group of a dozen men living in Jerusalem in
the first century AD. None of these societies, as Desmond Morris
points out, have been 'successful' in the modern technological sense
– but that may not be to their discredit.

Given that we haven't the faintest idea whether the optimists or
the pessimists are likely to be proved right in the Great Chips
Debate – or, come to that, in any of the other debates about the
future use of new technologies – what should we actually *do*? To
that, at least, there is one safe answer. If the optimists turn out to be
right, all will be well and we need do nothing – except to get on with
developing and applying the new technology. But they may be
proved wrong; so, for the event that the pessimists are making the
better forecasts, let us construct now all the social safeguards we can
think of to protect our descendants from *that* outcome – or at least
to mitigate its consequences for them. That will at least serve as
some protection against the worst. And if the time ever does come
where it is plain that the optimists' horse has irreversibly won, that
will be the time to dismantle the safeguards.

But not before: among baboons, the chimp is a very vulnerable
beast.

IT: Doom or boon

IT has been hailed as a Utopian panacea and as a nightmarish dystopia. IT will bring greater decentralisation, a reallocation of power from the hands of the few to the terminals of the many, more flexible working patterns and increased leisure. IT will bring more state control, a new class system based on access to information, invasion of privacy on an unprecedented scale, mass unemployment and social disintegration.

Chairman: David Firnberg. Speakers: Christopher Price, MP Shirley Williams, MP

THE BLACK, THE WHITE AND THE GREY

With such a sweeping title, this first section can only deal with generalities. But it quickly opens up the main underlying controversy. Chris Price, with an Orwellian scenario which he describes as 'wholly plausible', plays the role of the profound pessimist. Shirley Williams is far more opimistic: she describes at least some of the more constructive uses to which IT can be put. As professional legislators, both call for social regulation, in the form of laws to protect the citizen from abuse; their proposals are not very different, though neither of them gives much detail of what such laws might say, how they would work, and who would police and enforce them — except that Price, right at the start, puts forward a set of principles for data protection which are exactly the ones that are about to be enacted, even though he says that we are still 'a very long way' from them (see Chapter 4).

Many of their points were of course developed in greater detail in the later sessions. Meanwhile, here are some reactions of my own.

To me, Price's scenario raises a host of unanswered questions. Why should the citizens of one of the world's freest countries tamely allow some future government to institute such a totalitarian system of social control? Why should the Parliamentarians of that time tamely pass all the necessary legislation? Such things have happened often enough when a military dictatorship, or a dedicated revolutionary party, takes over all power within the state by force. But why should a mature representative parliamentary democracy suddenly become so craven? Surely not all MPs — let alone all their electors – would be so naive and stupid as to allow themselves to be conned by that old piece of doom-mongering about the 'crime wave'?

Price's faith in the better side of human nature seems to be as limited as his faith in the critical faculties of the electorate. To him, the spectre of the baboon looms always, chillingly, over the scene. But where has the chimpanzee disappeared to? It only makes a brief appearance at the end, as the protagonist of a 'convivial, open, socialist society'. But if the road to that is open today, why will it not still be open tomorrow? Will the forces of light suddenly vanish in a puff of electronic smoke, abandoning all they have achieved in innumerable battles against the forces of darkness over at least the last couple of centuries, if not far longer? To take just a small example, we *did* have identity cards during the Second World War, but we managed to get rid of them again. (True, that was not through any efforts by Parliament, but through a judgment in 1951 of the late Lord Chief Justice Goddard – not exactly renowned for his socialism, though he was certainly convivial. I've always regarded that as rather a triumph for the Rule of Law.)

Price raises an interesting question about unemployment, but unfortunately he doesn't pursue it very far. Let us suppose that IT, applied to industrial processes, continues to make them ever less labour-intensive. Let us also suppose that it creates no equivalent employment elsewhere. (The first of those suppositions is probable, the second much less so.) The result would be high unemployment, combined with high production of very cheap goods and services. Without anyone having to do much work, there would be more than enough to go around. But on what basis would we then distribute those goods? When Price's all-powerful state has given every family two free colour TV sets and a free motor car, who gets the third TV and the second car, which are still 'scarce' and so become status goods?

In the past (which was always one of scarcity), we adopted the principle 'to each according to his contribution' – work harder, and you will get a bigger share of what work produces. We have now tempered that with a welfare safety-net principle of 'to each according to his (basic) need'. But what happens when all basic needs are already satisfied, and contribution (in the form of work) is no longer necessary for production? Evidently, we shall need a new principle of distribution. But what will it be? To each according to his worth? Or merit? Or desert? And what will be the tests for these, and who will apply them? Put another way, what should be the differentials in unemployment benefits? Does the unemployed computer programmer get more than the unemployed factory cleaner?

Price foresees the allocation of some system of Brownie points by all-powerful government officials. That is always an unattractive prospect – though it happens all over the country even now, in the field of social security, municipal housing, education, and a host of other things. But how will it be done in the socialist society he wants to see established? If it's by direct local democracy, I don't fancy the prospects of unemployed urban blacks where they are in the minority – or of unemployed urban whites, or women, where *they* are. Otherwise, how else *can* it be done – except by laws, made by Parliament and administered by officials, which is precisely what we have now? Surely only baboons can *make* people behave like chimpanzees, if they are not *all* willing to do it by themselves.

Shirley Williams has more faith in the good sense and the constructive instincts and abilities of ordinary people – even if not of her colleagues in the present Parliament. Her idea of a return to pre-industrial-revolution work patterns is attractive. There is a submerged vision here of the benevolent master craftsman, surrounded by his apprentices as part of his extended family – until one remembers that those were the bad old days of feudalism, enclosures, and growing numbers of landless labourers and *their* families, with only the benevolence of the squire between them and the workhouse. But her emphasis on personal autonomy, self-reliance, and freely-chosen mutual cooperation for sharing and caring ends is crucial – on almost any rational view, those are the central things which any political or economic system *ought* to be designed to encourage.

Paul Sieghart

OUTLOOK DOOM: MYTH OR REALITY?
CHRISTOPHER PRICE MP

Put like this, the question is not a sensible one. Information technology is here and here to stay. It has economic advantages in a properly organised society. It can shorten working hours and make work more pleasant. It makes possible access to information at a speed and over a range never imaginable before. Like the telephone, it provides a quantum leap in communication.

Like all new inventions, however, it will be used by the powerful for the oppression of the weak. What I am advocating is a set of rules which can be enforced by individuals, whether employees or not, to try to ensure that computer-stored information about individuals is:
● accurate
● held by an organisation which has some need for it
● not so out of date as to be oppressive or meaningless
● protected from those who have no right to it
● available to the individual concerned.
We are a very long way from any such rules in Britain today.

Also, like all new inventions, information technology will cause massive disruption to patterns of work. It will create unemployment for the many and leisure for the few. We therefore need rules to ensure that working people gain the benefit from this technology and that it is not used simply to increase the differentials between the privileged employed and the underprivileged on the dole. We face the prospect of a population with greater surveillance from above and less satisfaction from below. IT can be a powerful instrument of repression. Today there is a desparate resolution on the part of the Western world not to face this problem or talk about it.

So − here's a quite plausible future for you and your children in a few years' time. Everyone over the age of five will have a plastic identity card. It will contain your photograph, fingerprints and a number. It will be very difficult to forge, since any policeman will be able to check the prints against the number at any police station. (The excuse for its gradual introduction will be the rising crime wave; Britain is one of the few European countries to have abolished the identity card after the Second World War. Most countries simply kept the Nazi-originated system they had inherited.) The authorities − policemen and others − specifically authorised by new security legislation (justified in Parliament by the rising political opposition to these new systems of repression) will have access to computer-stored information comprising your credit record, your payments of tax and social security contributions, your bank and credit card balances, your encounters with the police and the law (whether or not any criminal charges or convictions were involved), your physical and mental health record, details of all occasions on which you have entered or left the UK, your education and training qualifactions with the particular grades you received, your work record, including absences, warnings, reprimands and dismissals, your marital status, details of your children (both intra- and extra-marital) and such other information as it seems proper to the security authorities to store concerning you. It will be illegal to store personal information except against your identity number. Access to this information by other individuals and corporate bodies will be strictly controlled, in accordance with our treaty obligations in Europe. The police and the security services are not, however, covered by these restrictions. They will have (sometimes only at certain ranks and above) unlimited access.

In spite of legislation making it illegal to take paid employment except between the ages of 21 and 55 (with exceptions in the case of 'essential government staff' as designated by the Home Secretary by order), 65 percent of those adults eligible to register (a figure which will exclude a very large number of married women) will be unemployed, and receive benefit at an indexed rate sufficient for subsistence which will take account of housing, food, alcoholic drink and television needs. This subsistence rate will be available to all the unemployed (unless voluntarily so) and all students (except those designated as on courses of National Importance, who will receive 'enriched' grants). The main leisure industries will be television, radio and sport; current affairs programmes will be discouraged and strictly controlled.

Because of the crime rate, a curfew will be increasingly imposed after dark which will apply to all citizens except those allowed private transport, because of the essential nature of their work. Standards of education, health care and housing will be monitored and maintained, fuel prices will be held at a reasonable level, and though the subsistence level for the unemployed will be low, it will be very much higher than that of most of those in full time work in the Third and Fourth world. Every house will have a telephone, but all conversations will be recorded for perusal by the security services, and check words will enable them to extract politically sensitive conversations at a moment's notice. Cheap postal services will be available; all letters however will be read (unopened) electronically and the contents stored for spot checks. It will be compulsory to put the identity number of the sender on each item posted. Trade unions, religious bodies, charities of all sorts will be encouraged but will have to register themselves (and be alloted a number),their membership (with identity numbers) and their times of meetings so that an Authorised Person can attend if he or she so wishes. Because of the crime wave — and the need to check on all unauthorised gatherings — it will be a serious offence to hold a meeting of an unregistered association or any meeting at an unannounced time.

This is a wholly plausible scenario for which the technology already exists. It is unlikely to happen in Eastern Europe, because they are behind with the technology; it could not happen in the Third World because they could not afford it. If it happen anywhere, it will come first in Western Europe or North America. It will not happen all at once; but tension in other parts of the world, the need to maintain our arms industries to fuel that tension, the need to develop and protect nuclear power and the opposition this policy will generate, the political dissidence at home and above all, the massively mounting crime wave by those of the unemployed who opt for deviant rather than conformist behaviour will force democratically-elected politicians to adopt such methods as the only possible option. It will starkly divide society into two classes; the privileged in work and the underprivileged on subsistence benefit. The best paid jobs will be in multi-national companies, the armed forces, the civil service and the police; teachers and health workers will get lesser rewards and, because of fear of losing their jobs, will not be disposed to press for a higher status; the economic cycle will have become irrelevant to job opportunities — the progress of information and other technologies will be able to reduce permanently those employed to less than half of the population. Where the demand for labour-intensive industries arises, these will be carried on by the Western controlled multi-nationals in the poorest countries in the Fourth World.

It is possible for Western countries to guard against such natural developments. Briefly they will involve democratic control of the police and the security services, constitutional guarantees on privacy, the making of information gleaned in breach of such guarantees inadmissible in court; subject to the guarantees for personal privacy, entrenched clauses guaranteeing corporate (both government and private) openness and the freedom of the press; massive eroding of the differentials between the 'employed' and the 'unemployed', and indeed the discarding of such terms as pejorative of human beings and useless to describe the many non-work contributions which individuals provide for society; in short, rapid progress towards a convivial, open, socialist society. Lack of such guarantees and such progress will involve an inevitable slide into repression and fascism.

OUTLOOK BOON: REALITY OR MYTH?
SHIRLEY WILLIAMS

In a sense information technology deepens all our choices. It means that all our choices are known to a greater extent than they were before. We can choose the path towards a deliberate limitation of the state's power in a democracy, or we can move towards a tyrannical structure. Those choices become much more significant than before since if the wrong choices are made, then the significance of a wrong choice is greater than it used to be 40 or 50 years ago.

That is not to say that the coming of information technology has anything to do with the actual decision for tyranny or democracy, but information technology does give the state much bigger power if it wishes to exercise it — and it can make a tyranny an extremely efficient tyranny. A Soviet historian once said that liberty grows in the interstices of the state; in other words, the inefficiencies of the state are where liberty can survive, even if the state is an undemocratic one. Certainly inefficient tyrannies are much more possible to live in than efficient tyrannies. That is why Nazi Germany in the end was very much worse than fascist Italy.

Another danger that is implicit, not so much in information technology itself as in the possibility of a very wide range of cable television and broadcasting, is the demise of the public broadcasting system. The system which makes accessible to all people the most attractive events, whether they are the World Cup in football, or the premiere of a major play or a major concert, might no longer be available because the commercial competition of cable companies might simply knock to pieces the BBC and the whole structure of public service broadcasting.

A third danger is that the coming of information technology can create a new kind of class privilege. That has two spin-offs. One is geographical, which is why the New World Information and Communication Order has become a subject of massive interest to UNESCO. The fear of UNESCO is that an information technology dominated by the English-speaking Western countries (and English is the language of information technology) could deprive the southern hemisphere of its own access and control over information and data in a way that could create a new kind of very sophisticated imperialism. The second spin-off is that it could create generational divisions, between the old who do not understand computer languages, the role of the computer, data processing and all the rest of it, and the young who do and who are almost born to it. People in middle age are of course balanced on the point where they either try to understand the coming of the information revolution, or where they think it is all too wearisome and give up. So all these things should be considered because they are part of the significance of the decisions that we have to make.

Let us now turn to the prospects – and I think they are glittering and extremely exciting – of what information technology could mean to us if we use it properly. We have a fairly dread warning in the misuse of nuclear power. Nuclear power, rather like information technology, offered the same tremendous opportunities. There was the possibility of being able to harness a form of energy (I mean fusion, not fission) that would provide a relatively inexpensive and eternal source of power to an energy-hungry world. On the other side, there was the possibility of weapons of mass destruction – and sadly the world has put more resources into the second category than the first. That is an example of a technology which has raised the stakes, and which has essentially gone sour. It may be, if one has little faith in human nature, that that is the inevitable consequence of an advance in technology. I don't believe it is so.

Information technology could finally end the constraints and restraints of the first industrial revolution. It permits people who are at work to escape from the restraint that implied a work space and a work pattern for all those who sought work. The first industrial revolution gave birth to industrial antagonism, to the idea of industrial classes, and to the idea of the assembly line which was a higher form of serfdom. All this was implicit in the fact that the location of industry was imposed by the scale of industry, by the method and pattern of industry and by the fact that it was impossible for people to continue to work effectively from home.

Information technology breaks that link, and breaks it in two ways. First, it removes the locational constraints. It means that the travelling can be done by the electronics and not by the individual human being. It means that many people will escape from the tyranny of commuterism, from having to live within travelling distance of their work. And it means that many people who simply cannot get away from home for long periods, because of their responsibilities to members of the family, will be enabled to take part in the world of work and the whole community in a way they simply cannot do today.

Secondly, the new technology demands a much greater degree of independence and autonomy on the part of management and employees than the old technology. The best of the new technologies work most effectively in countries which are willing to accept single conditions of work, which are willing to reject hierarchy, which are willing to embrace industrial democracy and industrial consultation; and they work very badly in countries like our own which are locked into traditional patterns of industrial warfare. The second consequence, therefore, of information technology is that it is literally going to smash to pieces the hierarchical management structures that still characterise British industry.

Thirdly, information technology will enable us to use far more sensibly and economically the raw materials and energy which are clearly finite. For example, you can build information technology into transport in such a way as to minimise the waste of fuel. You can actually build into it, for example, immediate knowledge about any traffic blocks down the road and you can build in information about how to avoid those traffic blocks so as to use energy more efficiently. You can gear into machinery and into vehicles information that enables them to be run in a way that minimises energy use. You can use the power over numerically-controlled machine tools to reduce the use of metals and other finite raw materials by machining to much finer tolerances. That really seems to be a fundamental responsibility of the rich north towards the poor south, because at the moment the rich north simply absorbs raw materials and other resources of primary energy at a rate that means the rest of the world is being massively deprived.

There is in my view a massive revolution that could happen — though of course it might not. But let's look for a moment at the

potential. One could get a massive change in the way public services are run. Take the elderly, the disabled and the housebound. All are at the moment divorced from part of their community. When you are able to shop through a visual display on your own television set for the various things that you want; when you are able to be linked up by radio with a social worker who is immediately available to help and advise; when you are able to computer-control a car so that every day the visiting rota of district nurses can be organised in the most efficient possible way to give cover for emergencies and alarm calls — for a very wide range of housebound and disabled people you've moved into a different dimension of the welfare state. When you are able (as is happening already in the highlands of Scotland) to link up groups of elderly and housebound people with one another so as to create a new community in which they can participate and be, as it were, part of a communicating and co-operative life — then you've created a new dimension in the battle against loneliness. When, as presently in Warsaw, you link up the repair vans with the necessary equipment so that people repairing houses can move about efficiently without having to go back to base and waste a great deal of time getting stock from warehouses — then you are going to move into an area where people may be able to get much more rapid repair of their houses.

I don't accept some of the fears about unemployment. Take the example of the banking system in France and Germany. (It's a little too early to say anything about Britain's banking because we've only recently adapted ourselves to computer technology.) In Germany there has been an actual expansion: an increase in overall employment of about 30% and a wide range of customer services that did not exist before. My only objection to the introduction of computers in banking is that it makes most bank statements almost totally incomprehensible.

Assuming that information technology is accessible to most people, it is also going to open up new dimensions of control by the citizen of his or her own local and national government. But that hinges upon three pieces of legislation that are absolutely essential. First, we must lay down in Britain, which is the most secretive of so-called democratic societies in the western world, the right to all information that is not classified for the most overwhelming reasons. That means reforming the Official Secrets Act and pulling it back to the very minimum of secrecy that is required to protect national security and guard against foreign espionage. It means giving citizens the right to information outside that very narrow area.

Secondly, we need a Protection of Citizens Bill which covers not

only privacy but also such things as the intrusion of the press into people's lives. We ought to protect people's rights to get their own individual records, and we have to build in complete barriers between each computer data processing system in such a way that it is impossible for the police computer to get access to the National Health Service computer and for that to get access to the Inland Revenue computer without going through an open and elaborate process which would have to be individual; that is to say, each case would have to be made out on its merits. All this is possible. The Swedes have blocks built in between data processing systems and between computer storage systems. They have a citizens' group of ombudsmen whose job is to check constantly that these barriers are not broken.

A final piece of legislation that I would like to see would entrench the human rights of the individual in the non-existent British constitution (which means that it has to be a law binding on the courts) and make sure that the whole of the information revolution is bound and constrained by that.

One final thought — and it's a very important one and a very frightening one. The information revolution is coming very fast. The police have already gone a long way to establishing data systems; so has the National Health Service; and the Inland Revenue and the Social Services records will be computerised by 1985 or 1986. The worrying thing about Britain is that parliament has not moved to set up in parallel to the rapidity with which computerisation and data processing is arriving, a similar structure of controls and of protection for the individual citizen. The lesson we must draw from that is that we had better pick up our batons and start running very much faster. Information technology could bring a much better life for our people, but not if parliament insists on continuing slowly towards the end of the nineteenth century, having just moved from the quill pen to the fountain pen.

The Third World: Independence or dependence?

IT is more capital intensive than labour intensive. Will this negate the "Less Developed Countries (LDC's)" traditional advantages of cheap labour? Many LDC's do not have sufficiently comprehensive infrastructures to support IT. What problems will this create not only in terms of increased inequalities between First and Third World countries, but also in terms of inequalities between urban and rural communities inside the LDC's? The advance information of weather patterns etc. that IT can provide could radically improve the LDC's ability to plan agriculture, but while the possession and control of this information remains in the developed world, especially in the US, will its political price remain too high? What regulations can be used to control trans-border data-flow? Will IT destabilise already unstable LDC's political systems? Would the Ayatollah, for instance, have been able to depose the Shah of Iran from his base in Paris without the use of cassettes to influence the illiterate?

Chairman: Alan Benjamin. Speakers: Alan Benjamin, Juan Rada, Rita Cruise O'Brien

THE BALANCE OF POWERS

Just as IT can have profound effects on the relationships between individuals and groups *within* nations, so it can profoundly affect relationships *between* nations. Here again, it could be used to reduce unjust inequalities, or to increase them.

In this session, Juan Rada and Rita Cruise O'Brien play the role of the pessimists pointing out what is already bad, and how it is likely to get worse. Alan Benjamin is the lone optimist, giving examples of what has been done already, and of how other things could be done hereafter. Here are a few more of my own.

Information from satellites could be used to warn Bolivian farmers of approaching pests or climatic hazards – or it could be sold exclusively to acommodity broker who will make a killing out of buying that commodity forward. Given a simple terminal and a small dish aerial, an up-country doctor in Chad could find out everything that world medical science can tell him about the diagnosis and treatment of the patient he has in front of him at that moment — or he might be charged far more than he or the patient could ever afford as their contribution to the cost of putting all that information together in the first place. An engineer in Burma could use a microcomputer to design the simplest and cheapest bridge to cross his local river, and to produce a full schedule of the local materials he needs — if he can afford to buy or rent the machine and the necessary programs.

The problem here is not only the selfish desire of people who have useful knowledge to profit from it at the expense of others who have not. It is also deeply rooted in the very odd cost structure of IT.

The costs of IT

To put together software of any complexity — whether in the form of data or of programs — is a highly-skilled and still very time-consuming business. It is therefore very costly, as the experts who do it understandably insist on being well paid. So, for the same reason, is the design of the hardware (including, especially the chips), and the tooling-up for its manufacture. Once that heavy investment has been made, the *marginal* costs of producing each unit of hardware, and of running the software on it, are (by comparison) very low.

So, the *marginal* costs of supplying the necessary hardware to the Bolivian farmer, the Chad doctor or the Burmese engineer, and letting them run the highly sophisticated software on it, might well be low enough for them to be able to afford it. But the *total* cost (including their appropriate share of the huge design and development cost) would be far beyond their means. Yet, unless the producer can somehow recover that huge initial investment he will simply not make it, and there will be neither hardware nor software.

That of course is the principal reason why we have patents, copyrights, and other forms of 'intellectual property': without them, it would not be worth anyone's while to invent, write books or computer programs, compose music, paint, make films, or indeed do anything creative. Except, perhaps, for the pleasure and satisfaction of doing it — but then that applies to all work, and at the end of the day even those who enjoy their work somehow have to live.

However attractive it might therefore seem to charge users of information systems — especially those who most need them, but can least afford them — only the marginal cost, that could soon prove counterproductive: if the producer's incentive disappears, he will simply cease to create the necessary information, and the splendid new IT systems and channels will fall silent, devoid of the only material they were constructed to produce and distribute.

Market or regulation?

So what is to be done? The two classical solutions to such problems are the free market, or the regulated economy. The free market may have many virtues, but one of its most obvious features is that it favours the strong and drives out the weak: indeed, that is precisely what it is designed to do, and praised for doing by its proponents. In a free information market, the Third World could easily lose out: it starts from an initial position so disadvantaged that, unaided, it could probably never grow to compete on equal terms.

One is therefore left with the option of some form of regulation. That presents rather different problems, for who is to make and apply the regulations? There is as yet no such thing as a supra-national state, enjoying a monopoly of power over the sovereign nations. (If there ever were, by the way, it would almost certainly be authoritarian, if not overtly fascist, since there is no way in which it could be made directly accountable to the world's peoples, as opposed to their governments.)

Lacking such means of enforcement, international regulation can only come about, and remain in place, by the continuing consent of *all* those who are to be subjected to it. And why should those who appear to have something to lose from such regulation consent to anything of the kind – unless, that is, they get something of at least equal value in return?

For the richer democratic countries, the problem is in one sense even worse. Ministers – and we have had some – may be perfectly willing to spend public money on aid to poor countries. But that money can only come from taxes, and if the electorate disagrees with that allocation it will not vote for that Minister or his party again, and he will find himself out of office while his successor tightens the reins. So the question is: are there votes for helping the Third World? In some countries like Sweden, there undoubtedly are. In the UK, there are sadly few – as several politicians have found to their cost. However much people may sympathise with the Third World's poor, few are willing to give up their jobs for them, or – more likely these days – take cuts in their unemployment pay at their own families' expense.

Aid and trade

There is of course the argument from enlightened self-interest, as developed most persuasively by the late Barbara Ward, and by the Brandt Report. That excellent book sold more copies in the UK than in any other country. But any effect it might have had on public attitudes – at least as expressed at the polling stations – still remains to be seen.

Aid to the Third World also presents a few other problems. For a start, it doesn't always reach the rural poor in those countries for whom it is intended: too often, it goes to build grandiose industrial monuments to the current political leaders. Next, it is still far too often 'tied', either visibly or invisibly, to the commercial or strategic interests of the donor nations. Finally, it can prove very costly to the receiving countries themselves: even at favourable interest rates, many of them now have to pay out all their foreign exchange earnings from their exports just to service their loans. Indeed, more than one such country is now technically bankrupt, and saved from being put into receivership only by the fact that this is something the international community simply cannot afford to do to an independent nation. And that is now putting the world's entire financial system at risk.

No wonder the Third World is calling for a New International Economic Order. That idea in fact has a good deal of support from the developed countries, including the UK. But it is still a very long way from actually being installed in real life. Meanwhile, many millions more will starve, or eke out a meagre and deprived living – while even the poorest among us here is, by their standards, living the life of Riley.

In this part of the field, the outlook is probably more depressing than in any other.

Paul Sieghart

A THIRD WORLD PERSPECTIVE
DR JUAN RADA

Technology has played a crucial role in the economic, social and political developments of the past two centuries, whether they be national or international.

It is clear that changes in technology deeply affect the worldwide distribution of productive facilities and services, and the international division of labour. A classic example of socio-economic and technical change that has profoundly altered human existence is, of course, the Industrial Revolution, which was brought about, among other things, by technological advances in textile manufacturing. These advances changed the international division of labour for textiles. By the 1830s the price of yarn was perhaps one twentieth of what it had been 50 years earlier, and the cheapest Hindu labour could not compete in either quality or quantity with

Lancashire's mules and throstles.

This example illustrates the interaction between technical change and the international division of labour. Today's situation is, however, rather different due to the characteristics and nature of microelectronics. These differences challenge the traditional conception of technology, development and industrialisation.

The importance of technology for development and for a more equitable world system is commonly recognised today. The control of technology often means the control of development, the definition of its aims and even its pace.

To assess the impact of technological changes, it is necessary to look at the inequalities within and among nations. In information technology, at least three different areas of inequality are apparent.

The first is in the distribution of *scientific and technological capabilities*. Developing countries account for around 3% of the world's total expenditure on science and technology, and they possess only 13% of the world's scientists and engineers. Even these figures are deceptively high, however; the lion's share is concentrated among a few developing countries, such as India, Brazil, Argentina and Mexico.

The second area of inequality is in *industrial capability*. In 1973, the United Nations Industrial Development Organisation (UNIDO) set an industrialisation goal for the Third World which became known as the Lima Target. It said that the developing countries should increase their share of the world's industrial output from 7% to at least 25% by the year 2000. By 1980, this share had hardly reached 9% and, unless special steps are taken, it will not exceed 13% by the end of the century.

The third area of inequality is in the *information infrastructure* of societies. In developing countries, according to UNESCO, one person in 30 gets a daily newspaper and only one in 500 has a television set. In contrast, the figures for the developed countries are one in 3 and one in 12, respectively. And the gap is now widening rapidly as the information infrastructure becomes more and more electronic. In data processing equipment, the consulting firm Diebold (Europe) estimates that the USA, Japan and Western Europe accounted for 83% (by value) of the world total in 1978. The share held by the rest of the world will have risen only marginally by 1988 — to 20%. Large Western banking firms possess more computer power than the whole of India. In telecommunications equipment, the developing countries represented 10% of the world market (including telephones) in 1980, and will represent only 14% by 1990.

This huge gulf between the industrialised countries and the

Third World is only part of the story, however; there are also enormous inequalities within and among the developing countries themselves. The term "developing countries" includes many different levels of economic, social, political and cultural development – though often with a similar colonial history and many common interests. These differences make generalisations hazardous and possibly misleading.

In many of these countries, electronic products reach no more than a tiny minority: the urban upper class and some sections of the middle class. The overwhelming majority of the people does not feel the impact or reap any benefits. While the advanced world is moving towards integrating thousands of conventional electronic components on a single silicon chip, in Africa only one person out of 18 has a radio; the transistor revolution, which spearheaded today's electronics nearly 30 years ago, has not yet arrived there.

All this points to the fact that the underlying socioeconomic, cultural and political reality of the world is not only increasing in complexity, but also widening the gap between rich and poor. Although there is no easy diagnosis or answer to the dilemmas posed for developing countries by rapid and different technological change, there are some fundamental issues that need urgent attention if a proper perspective of the challenge ahead is to be acquired.

Two other important elements must be mentioned. The first is the increasingly tough attitude that Western countries are adopting as a result of their own painful process of adjustment. The second is that as microelectronics expand and develop, they need a world market because of the huge investment in capital, research and development needed to make their producers truly competitive. So although developing countries, in many cases, represent a very small market, they are nevertheless important for making investment worthwhile. Underlying this is the fact that electronic component, computer and telecommunications technology is concentrated in the hands of a few transnational companies. As national economies become more dependent on these technologies, the power of these companies, already great, will increase, leading to yet greater dependence.

The impact of microelectronics
There are five main areas where developing countries will be affected by microelectronics:
1. Comparative advantages are increasingly dependent on science and technology, rather than accidents of geography or history. This is not to say that the latter will not remain important, particularly in relation to raw materials and energy. But as far as production (and

not only manufacturing) is concerned, comparative advantage will
be determined more and more by scientific and technological know-
how. Traditional industries are moving towards high technology,
and this shift will increase the gap between nations.

2. The cost of labour is becoming a less important part of total
manufacturing costs. In a number of industries this has already
reduced the developing countries' advantage of abundant low-cost
labour. It is the continuation of a trend which first became apparant
in agriculture. A massive return of industry to the advanced countries is unlikely. But the present international division of labour will
probably remain comparatively stable, with some return in certain
sectors. This has serious implications for the Third World's plans to
develop its industry.

3. Production is increasingly the result of capital investment rather
than the use of labour. A classic example is modern agriculture,
where unequal access to capital has led to wide disparities within
and between countries.

In developing countries, modern technology is confined to an
enclave, geared in most cases to export markets. This increases the
dislocation among advanced, less-advanced and traditional technologies. A polarisation of skills takes place, not only at the factory
level, but also on the international scale, as the suppliers of equipment are mostly in developed countries.

The more intensive use of capital raises the old question about
employment. The introduction of computers and information technology in developing countries could bring an immediate loss of
existing jobs and hamper the creation of new ones, particularly if
these countries are not producers or assemblers of equipment.
However, the impact on jobs may be relatively less important than
in the developed countries. On present trends, other technologies
like the mechanisation of agriculture are much more important in
terms of employment. More than the use of the technology itself,
the erosion of comparative advantages and the change in the nature
of the productive infrastructure have a far greater effect on jobs,
especially in view of the calculation by the International Labour
Office that 625 million new jobs have to be created in the Third
World in the last quarter of this century.

4. The trend towards combining more and more functions in a single
electronic component has important repercussions for developing
countries. One of their main strategies for absorbing foreign technology has been to "unpack" it, by dividing its various processes
and products into separate parts and sub-stages. That now becomes
increasingly difficult as technology is "packaged" or "frozen" into
the components themselves.

5. the production of goods and services depends increasingly on efficient processing and access to informations. The so-called "information-intensive" industries, like data processing and information services of a scientific, technical or commercial nature, are heavily concentrated in advanced countries. this poses questions of great importance for developing countries, both economically and culturally. For instance, the use of data bases implies the need to import services and − in most cases − the hardware to receive the services. And to some extent it also involves importing cultural patterns and interpretations.

These five main areas of concern are less applicable to those countries which do not have an industrial base, or even the beginnings of one. But they should know what the choices are and understand the dynamics of industrialisation. Before a country can make use of information technology it needs an adequate infrastructure, a regular electricity supply and fairly sophisticated telecommunications (which in most developed countries are taken for granted). But even in the least-developed countries, useful and practical applications for microelectronics can be found − especially in agriculture. Nevertheless, the benefits of the new technology must be measured by the national capacity to absorb its applications, rather than by the simple importation of complete systems. Furthermore, if advanced technological innovations increase the inequalities within countries, they will not help development but hinder it.

Although the current changes have negative effects which are difficult to adjust to, they also offer many opportunities. Equipment which has skills built into it, such as precision machinery, removes the need for human skills which are often difficult and costly to acquire. As a result, in some precision engineering activities (where labour will be needed in great quantities) new opportunities to leapfrog traditionally low and medium-grade mechanical skills have become available.

Consumer electronics and components

Since different countries follow different development strategies, generalisations are hazardous. Here, we shall concentrate on a handful of developing countries which have sought export-led growth. They are not typical, but they do illustrate very forcefully and clearly the dilemma facing developing countries.

To a greater or lesser extent, all countries want to diversify from agriculture and raw materials production into manufactured and semi-manufactured products. The route they take ranges from strict import substitution to fairly open economies with free zones to attract foreign companies.

For countries in the latter category, electronics has been a substantial part of their overall strategy because, in the past, the industry used a lot of labour for assembly and needed small amounts of capital per worker. These countries, particularly in South-East Asia, have now upgraded electronics in an effort to diversify towards high quality products, increasing the level of nationally-produced components in the finished goods.

The intense competition in electronics has led to constant cost-cutting and rapid innovation. It was largely in order to cut costs that many firms in advanced countries moved their assembly work overseas during the 1960s and early 1970s. The trend now, however, is to site new plants in the advanced countries. Reasons include: automation, the need to be closer to customers, quality control, elimination of logistical problems, and the need to upgrade local or national capabilities. Since 1978, the major investment in semiconductor plants has been in Europe, Japan and the US. At the same time, offshore installations are being moved from high-cost Asian countries – such as Singapore, Hong Kong, Taiwan and South Korea – to countries like Thailand and the Philippines in an effort to cut costs further. In other cases, offshore plants are being automated.

This trend is reinforced by several factors, ranging from the desire of industrialised countries' governments to ensure a microelectronic base, to protectionist measures and currency values. But above all, the growing integration of electronic components and the automation of the manufacturing process mean that labour costs are not an over-riding consideration.

For Japanese producers, the use of offshore plants represents only about 10% of production, and in some areas it is declining. One factor of importance to the Japanese is the concern for quality, which they feel cannot be sufficiently maintained in offshore installations.

In the light of these changes, countries which rely heavily on foreign investment and imported technology in the electronics industry are becoming more vulnerable. The rapid pace of change could bring technological discontinuity, with severe effects on the industry. Products which are still labour-intensive in the assembly stage have lost an important part of their value-added elements due to the changes in components. For instance, the number of parts in television sets has been halved since 1970, eliminating much assembly work.

Today, advanced electronic technology – mainly concentrated in American and Japanese firms – is obtainable for the most part

only through co-production, joint ventures and cross-licensing. Transnationals generally make no systematic effort to encourage local research and development (R&D) or to re-invest profits beyond the minimum needed to keep the plant running. Governments therefore need to seek greater local R&D content while at the same time encouraging closer links between technical institutions and local firms. As technology becomes the basic asset of companies, their willingness to transfer it will decrease even further. Besides, transfer of technology is possible only if the human resources are there to absorb it. Even developing countries which are advanced in electronics, such as South Korea, had only 4 researchers per 10,000 of population in 1978, compared with 26 and 24 in the US and Japan respectively (in 1977). Spending on R&D per researcher is about $21,500 in Korea, compared with $47,560 in Japan and $80,680 in the US.

There is no doubt that some developing countries will eventually absorb part of the technology in specialised areas. Whether that will give them any significant stake in the international market for components and equipment is another matter.

As the speed of technological change increases, so does the need to spend money on investment and research. According to the Organisation for Economic Cooperation and Development, already by 1975 industries producing electrical and electronics machinery, equipment and supplies (including computers and related products) were the largest users of R&D, outstripping the chemical and aerospace industries. Many other areas not accounted for in the electrical groups, such as aerospace and machinery, are in fact heavily based on electronics, and considerable R&D efforts are undertaken. In addition, production support, in-company training, management development, and other items which are part of the technological environment are not accounted for, although they may have a significant impact on results.

It was around 1975 that rapid technological change and keen competition led to an acceleration in R&D expenditure by the electronics industry. The ten most important independent semi-conductor firms in the US more than doubled their R&D budgets, from more than $200 million in 1975 to more than $550 million in 1980. These figures exclude programmes from outside contractors such as the US government. In addition to company investments, the governments of the advanced countries have invested more than $3 billion since 1975 to finance R&D, and to manufacture and promote electronics.

In 1965 a typical production line for integrated circuits cost about $1 million. In 1980, due to the complexity of the circuits and automation, the cost ran as high as $40-$50 million. The combined effects of growing expenditure on R&D and capital investment have resulted in a concentration of business and technology which further polarises the international division of labour.

Some plants will stay in developing countries. Their task will be mainly the encapsulating, wiring and testing of components but sophisticated wafer fabrication will remain in the developed countries, particularly the US and Japan. There are three main reasons why a massive repatriation of offshore assembly work is unlikely in the medium term. First, under financial stress companies prefer to maintain offshort installations and put up with reduced profits rather than incur the cost of new investment. Secondly, labour laws often permit working conditions that are not tolerated in the developed countries. Thirdly, there is great pressure by governments in South-East Asia to maintain facilities, and up-grade technology.

One area where some developing countries could play an important role is software – providing they have a degree of speci-alisation and a forceful government policy. Software is a complex skill, but extremely labour-intensive. India, with its large propor-tion of highly educated people and its low labour costs, has success-fully exported software to developed countries. However, the sub-stitution of imported software could have an important effect on economy and employment. The clear distinction between software and hardware is, nevertheless, becoming increasingly untenable as more software is incorporated into chips and the components themselves become systems. The full control of the technology, therefore, will in the long run require proficiency in both aspects.

Information flows and developing countries

Much of the world's computer power and information processing industry is in the advanced countries, particularly the US. This concentration reinforces the imbalance between developed and developing countries.

For the developing countries, in addition to the cost of imported computing services, there is a loss of control over the direction of future economic and social developments because of the exodus of key decision-making processes. Furthermore, due to the decreasing cost of communications and the concentration of "information-intensive" sectors in developed countries, it is becoming cheaper in many cases for Third World enterprises and institutions to send their design problems, calculations, research and routine data abroad rather than assemble and develop local teams.

What happens, in fact, is a sort of "electronic brain-drain". The economies of scale achieved by information centres in developed countries make them very competitive internationally. Brazilian officials have stated that "dumping" of cheap time-sharing services has discouraged the establishment of this type of service within Brazil.

Trans-border data flows have created the potential for greater dependence, and with it the danger of losing legitimate access to vital information affecting economic and social developments. This has important political implications. There is a real risk of retention or selective release of data under conditions of economic war, or deteriorating international relations, for example. Some balance between imports and exports of data is required − a fact which needs to be considered by countries which are just establishing international data links.

The diffusion of information technology in developing countries resembles the general pattern found in Western countries, but has its own characteristics. The most visible aspect of this diffusion is the growing use of computers, although other types of equipment are being introduced.

Today the computer population and telecommunications capacity in developing countries are only a small fraction of the world total. At the same time, many products, notably capital goods, are being transformed by microelectronics. This in turn is influencing manufacturing processes.

There are several practical factors that slow down the rate of diffusion. One is labour costs, particularly in the use of computers for conventional purposes. Cheap labour makes the equipment less competitive. The lack of standardisation in a number of activities has made software requirements more demanding, so that the total cost of installations is more expensive than it would have been otherwise. Ready-made software "packages", even in the banking sector, are difficult to implement.

Trade unions have not been significant in acting as a brake, although examples of industrial action over computerisation exist in several countries.

The single most important factor affecting diffusion of the technology is undoubtedly government action. An increasing number of countries have adopted centralised systems to process import requests, monitor applications and purchase equipment for government needs.

On balance, a relatively rapid diffusion can be foreseen in computers and telecommunications, and in some industrial applications. But this does not necessarily imply that developing countries will be able to absorb microelectronic technology at a pace that will enable them to compete with the industrialised countries. They lack the awareness, skills and capital requirements. In this respect, developing countries are bound to benefit less from current changes.

Employment prospects

Although the effect of information technology on employment has been at the centre of the debate in the developed countries, the issue is rather different for developing countries. This is due to the structure of the labour market and to widespread uneremployment.

Some industries will choose developing countries as sites for establishing industries based on the new technology. the decision will be influenced less by low labour costs than by tax advantages, lack of labour resistance, lower start-up costs and cheaper capital. It is doubtful, however, whether this type of modern installation will create significant employment or contribute to the general development of the economy.

The result could be islands of high-technology within economies characterised by low-productivity and artisan-based production systems.

The industrial and service structure in most developing countries is sharply divided between a modern sector and a multitude of small businesses with extremely low productivity and high underemployment. A reduction of jobs or loss of potential employment in the "formal" sector increases pressure in the "informal" one, provoking further underemployment or unemployment there. This reinforces the pattern of low productivity and further inhibits economic growth. Thus the introduction of advanced technology has a chain effect and cannot be analysed only at the level of the individual enterprise using it. This aspect is particularly important when the equipment is imported and does not enhance internal manufacturing capabilities.

Studies in developing countries on the employment effects of computerisation tend to agree that there is a loss of potential employment, although initially some jobs in data processing are created. A similar pattern occurred in the early stages of computerisation in the advanced countries, but changes in input techniques (which are replacing key-punch operators) will diminish the level of job creation in the future. Furthermore, most developing countries import the equipment and thus no employment is created at the manufacturing or assembly level.

For some developing countries the combination of high technology and low labour cost, particularly of educated labour, could be one of the opportunities to develop an embryonic information industry and thereby to create employment. Already low-cost, highly qualified manpower is being used in a number of areas such as civil engineering, the provision of technical services in health, finance, and agriculture, and consultancies in general.

Whether these opportunities can be increased will depend on developments in software. Software will remain for some time a labour and skill intensive activity, so the low cost of labour can continue to be a comparative advantage in this area. Such an advantage depends on the country's current endowment of software skills and its capacity to keep software specialists at home.

Information technology and development

Information technology is a reality, and a rapidly expanding one. Therefore, the question is how to master the changes and deal with the issues it raises to the best advantage for development strategies. It will be necessary to learn how to harness current changes, while avoiding the undesirable effects of the technology. Microelectronics-based innovations can be of great benefit, if properly applied.

Three general principles apply to the use of the technology within countries. The first is the need for a national policy based on a careful selectiveness in applications. This should be aimed at overcoming bottlenecks and optimising the use of resources, rather than using the technology to replace labour, or to increase efficiency which could be increased by other means.

Second is the need to assure diversified sources of supply and to avoid becoming dependent on a few companies.

The third need is to monitor the national integration of locally assembled or partly manufactured electronic-based products. In general, countries use an index combining weight/volume/value to measure how much of a given product is nationally made. Integrated circuits, which are the heart of electronic-based products, have a very low weight/volume/value but they incorporate all the 'real' value of the product from the point of view of technology and know-how. If the purpose of a country is to up-grade its own national capability slowly in this area, it is important to monitor national integration in the light of changes in the technology.

Computer technology has long been used by government services in developing countries, especially for statistical purposes. This use could increase further, improving the accuracy, reliability and timing of statistical information. The time lag between events or policy implementation and their proper evaluation can be shortened considerably, thus increasing the efficiency of decisions, policy design and the monitoring of the performance of different measures.

With a solid information base, the technology can be used to optimize the allocation and use of resources, which in itself could mean considerable economies. A tighter control of commercial stocks, imports and exports, and tax collection could be of great benefit, while saving foreign exchange in many areas.

Although employment could increase marginally when new or supplementary services are created, in general the technology will diminish job creation potential. Thus a careful evaluation is needed to combine traditional and modern methods with desirable information and employment results. Countries can improve their planning and bargaining capacity if they are capable of assembling the information relevant to their interests. Other important applications are those which enhance social services, particularly health and education.

A call for action

Collective action should be taken in three main areas:

1. Joint efforts to develop technological and scientific assessment and forecasting in those areas most likely to have a profound effect on developing countries and the international division of labour.

2. Joint efforts to evolve a common information policy. This policy should encompass data banks, bases and networks in the economic, science and technology, research and development, cultural and mass media fields. The Third World should also evolve a common

policy towards communications, trans-border data flows, satellite links, and the transfer of technology. It should develop common facilities on a regional basis, with special emphasis, at least initially, on software.

3. Joint efforts to obtain preferential treatment for access to data banks and bases as a way to narrow the growing gap between developed and developing countries in areas such as science and technology.

It is necessary to warn that for the Third World, the potential benefits of the new technology remain largely on paper. They require an active search for alternative development strategies and this, ultimately, is related to the power structure within and between countries. If that structure is not altered in most countries and internationally, there is little hope that desirable benefits will materialise.

Data, information and a new productive infrastructure should not benefit only the few. We cannot have a world divided between information 'poor' and 'rich'. Data and information should not be used to infringe a people's cultural identity and invade, by means of different lifestyles, patterns of consumption and values, a world that is struggling to reach its own identity and development path.

More than legislation and protocols, a new atmosphere of social command of technologies should be developed. In this atmosphere, discussion about the use of technologies could take place. The wonders of current change could be used to solve pressing needs, for the benefit of all, in a more interdependent rather than dependent world.

NEW PROBLEMS IN NORTH-SOUTH RELATIONS
RITA CRUISE O'BRIEN

A crucial question for developing countries is how power over resources may be converted into power over events. Good access to information — and an ability to control that information — during negotiations is an important factor of power; poor access to information tends to incur present and future costs for the more vulnerable parties. It was in part because of lack of access to information, or poor organisation and use of information, that the South — that is, the world's poorest countries — achieved so little during the 1970s.

It is already apparent that information is a political issue. And this is a growing source of concern to US policymakers[1]: "Trade doesn't follow the flat any more," according to a member of the US mission to the Organisation for Economic Co-operation and Development, "it follows the communication system"[2].

Worldwide, information issues may be characterised in terms of "protectionism" versus the "free flow of information". As in the analagous case of international trade, national interests and the interests of transnational business line up differently on these issues. For example:

1. Satellites can analyse agricultural and mineral resources in great detail. The first American satellite designed for this purpose, Landsat 1, was launched in 1972[3]. Landsat 4, due to be launched this year (1982), will be ten times better and capable, for example, of observing agricultural output field by field.

Clearly, such information is invaluable to any country which can obtain it − and, as it happens, this particular information is available in digital form, free of charge, to anyone who asks for it. The snag is that it is of little use to those who lack the equipment and expertise to translate the sattelite's bleeps into detailed maps.

The gap between those who can and those who cannot interpret the data is especially important in agricultural commodity markets (coffee, cocoa, soya, etc.). Here, the considerable resources of private firms like commodity dealers can place less well-informed developing countries at a potentially serious disadvantage.

Data gathering by satellite raises a new series of questions about sovereignty and dissemination, already noted by the Soviet Union as well as Third World countries[4]. As the future of geo-politics is so intimately linked with strategic food resources, this may become of increasing importance.

2. The flow of information across national borders has become a major new issue. Data on markets, technology and credit assessments − all vital to the success of private firms − carry a potentially high market value. The worry is that the USA's near-monopoly of data bases and equipment may become a source of monopoly power and pose a further challenge to sovereignty. Already, several European countries have restricted the outward flow of information, and some newly-industrialising countries have introduced similar restrictions[5]. International businesses are quite concerned about these developments because, in their view, such moves seriously restrict the environment in which they seek to operate.

3. Telecommunications policy is also beginning to alarm the Third World. The body which controls access to channels of communication is the International Telecommunications Union, and there are signs that some of its newer member-countries may soon be

questioning its very structure. The first important meeting at which the South took an active interest in policy was the World Administrative Radio Conference (WARC) of 1979 which reallocated radio wavelengths for the first time in 20 years[6]. Previously, tariffs and channel allocations had been decided easily because there were still plenty of frequencies to spare and allocations were made on a first-come, first-served basis.

Now, however, the system which has guided and managed international telecommunications in the past is increasingly regarded as inadequate[7]. But although developing countries are aware of the problem, their limited capacity to put their cases effectively in the face of much greater expertise among business and government representatives is still a major barrier to change.

There is one slightly hopeful prospect, though. The lengthy deliberations of the WARC meant that discussion of some important matters had to be postponed, which may allow developing countries more time to assess their needs and obtain better briefing on technical details.

Information and negotiation

Some countries of the South have recently tried to alter international economic relationships through nationalisation, the exercise of greater control over exports and imports, etc. Such moves in turn alter their information needs. They must take difficult decisions on how much to spend, and in what ways, in order to improve the effectiveness of national participation in international bargaining.

This raises the question of whether the informationally weak have the capacity to acquire and process the information they now need to make decisions which are in their own interests, rather than in the interests of the larger information systems of which they previously formed part.

Knowledge of specialised markets is an essential need for successful bargaining. And yet many of the poorer countries have become involved in forms of market management over which they have lost significant control because of their lack of information on pricing, etc. They lack not only information, but information on where to acquire information.

At present information useful for trade reaches the developing countries' decision-makers through a wide variety of channels. Some is gathered by overseas commercial representatives, attachés, or agents. Some is assembled through trade journals, specialised consultancies, brokers and dealers, the messages of salesmen and foreign aid or trade bureaucrats, and various informal contacts[9]. Rarely is its assembly and dissemination systematised, as it normally is in large commercial enterprises[10]. In the poorest countries, the basic informational resources of libraries, data banks and the like are hopelessly inadequate; often they consist of nothing more than published material arriving sporadically by sea mail to under-staffed institutions[11]. Meanwhile, in the industrialised countries, the linking of computerised data banks and telecommunications facilities has dramatically altered the business information environment.

Still greater problems arise for developing countries in deciding how to make information effective when applied to specific problems; and their disadvantage is greatest of all in making information available in usable form at vital points in negotiation or decision-making.

It is the application of knowledge and organisation, skill and planning in the use of information which may be the most crucial factor in achieving a negotiating advantage. The capacity to organise information in terms which are appropriate may be most effectively achieved by buying-in outside expertise. Developing countries can do this either through United Nations agencies (or other forms of multilateral or bilateral aid), or through hiring the services of consulting firms like the Commodities Research Unit or Chase Econometrics.

At present, however, little is known about the advantages and limitations of using outside expertise in negotiation[12]. While it does ensure a greater flow of information, there is considerable difference in the capacity to use the information effectively among, say, copper transnationals like Anaconda and Kennecot, and producing countries with limited expertise like Zambia.

Some initiatives by institutions have been aimed at improving the negotiating capacity of developing countries. Specialised courses and conferences have been developed by the Centre for Transnational Corporations, UNCTAD, the International Legal Centre, the Commonwealth Secretariat, and UNIDO. There are also data banks designed to reduce the information gap of developing countries. Until recently, their main value was in project design where there is no time constraint, or in providing background information for research related to national decision-making and the improvement of applications for aid. Lately, however, there has been a growth in data on international finance and trade, through a system funded by the UN.

DEVSIS (International Development Research Centre, Canada) is intended mainly to assist the design of development projects. UNISIST (UNESCO) helps developing countries to establish their own information systems for use in national and local planning. The UNIDO system provides retrieval of information on industrial design, both at sectoral and plant level. The Development Information Network (UNDP, New York) provides financial and trade information but there is no memory for examining long-term trends.

The main problem with these systems is that they are underused. One of the reasons is that their information is generalised rather than specific; they try to serve everybody and end up serving almost nobody. In contrast, systems built around international professional groups, like the data banks of INIS (nuclear sciences) or AGRIS (agriculture) serve specific research needs and are much more effectively used.

There is also a danger that the UN and others may create data banks without taking into account professional capacity for decoding, synthesis and the use of information for sectoral needs. Inordinate amounts of money may be spent on establishing large prestige systems which are hardly used at all where the needs are greatest. For the purposes of negotiation (among other things) it may be essential to have information which is related to specific geographical areas. And there is a considerable difference in efficiency between information intended for particular users and that which can be effectively derived from data banks[13]. Thus, although most data banks aim to be as relevant as possible, they are inevitably not specific enough for most business and other negotiations.

New systems: new forms of disadvantage?

The fundamental question is what these new developments in the information industry hold for the future of North-South relations. Will the control of information become even more centralised than at present in traditional world centres, thus further enhancing the power and leverage of industrialised countries? Or will the developing countries (individually or in groups) be able to marshal and use new developments to reduce their present informational disadvantage?

The answer depends largely on the time-scale to be considered and on the capacity of systems to relate available information to specific needs. In the short term, technological developments may increase the power of already data-rich countries and firms. For the present, commercial incentives dictate the design of new equipment and systems – and the largest markets are private firms and carriers, and governments in industrialised countries. Transnational corporations depend on global "telematics" systems to increase their manoeuvrability in their relationships with governments, suppliers and customers. It is acknowledged in the business literature[14] that wider use of these systems will enhance the power and influence of these companies in relation to governments, and that it will widen the gap between rich and poor.

The major transnational corporations are far ahead, even of Western governments, in their use of the most modern information systems. Such firms have the capacity not only to use the new hardware of the data processing industry but also to develop, or encourage others to develop, the even more important software, the filtering and screening mechanisms which sift out the information they want[15]. This software is often designed for a specific industry or even a specific firm. Market incentives are, as always, guiding further technological developments in information processing. For computer firms,

> the large multinational firms with widely scattered operations represent the most attractive customers, so that enormous investments are being made to develop new applications and capabilities that would appeal to these firms. Further, the computer industry itself is becoming more unified through the use of common procedures, systems and software[16].

Modern telecommunications have thus evolved under US leadership, specifically to meet the needs of transnational corporations (and defence surveillance).

Transnational enterprise depends on the free flow of information across open borders. Since the end of the 1960s, the reduction of non-technical barriers like tariffs has led to an immense growth in private telecommunications carriers, upon which many forms of transnational enterprise now depend. These tendencies have led some analysts to ask whether the international information policy-making process has been able to cope with technological breakthroughs which promote increased interdependence.

Few have asked the basic question: In whose interests and at what cost?

Notes

1. See Glen O. Robinson, ed. *Communications for Tomorrow: Policy Perspectives for the 1980s*, New York: Praeger Special Studies and the Aspen Institute, 1978.
2. Report for the US Senate Foreign Relations Committee, *The New World Information Order*, November 1977.
3. William Lazarus, *Landsats, Minerals and Developments: A Quantitative Notion of the Downside Risk*, Occasional Papers, MIT Research Programme on Communication Policy, 1981.
4. Sensitivity to the issues of sovereignty and satellite communication had been apparent in connection with direct broadcast satellites from the early 1980s. See, K.M. Queeney, *Direct Broadcast Satellites and the United Nations*, The Netherlands: Sijthoff and Noordhoff, 1978.

5. Algeria, for example, allows no transmission of computer data to other countries. John Chippenger, "Who Gains from Telecommunication Development", unpublished report, Programme on Information Resources Policy, Harvard University, 1976.
Brazil requires the registration of foreign data links and Mexico has introduced conditions on foreign data flow. Details of these issues are summarised in the quarterly publication *Transnational Data Report*, Vols. 1-2, 1978-9 (Amsterdam).

6. The radio frequency spectrum is now recognised as a limited natural resource, which had previously not been challenged in terms of access for commercial, state or military needs. In 1979, developing countries laid claim to as much of the non-broadcast spectrum as they can be demanding "parking slots" which they could not yet use. The development of better bargaining capacity as well as resource allocation to national planning in this area is crucial to the protection of developing countries' interests.

7. H.K. Jackson, "ITU: a Pot-pourri of Bureaucrats and Industrialists" in R. Cox and H.K. Jackson, eds. *The Anatomy of Influence*, New Haven, Yale University, Press, 1973.

8. See R. Murray, ed. *Multinationals beyond the Market*, Intra-firm Trade and the Control of Transfer Pricing, Sussex: The Harvester Press, 1981.

9. UNIDO, for example, provides a series of Guides to Information Sources in such sectors as the machine-tool or fertiliser industry, or industrial quality control. Each gives directories of professional, trade and research organisations, sources of statistics, marketing and other economic data, but it is unclear how many developing countries actually make adequate use of such data.

10. See, for example, Paul A. Strassman, "Managing the costs of Information", *Harvard Business Review*, September-October, 1976.

11. These information problems can also directly affect the conduct of foreign policy. See, for example, Basil A. Ince, "The Information Gap and Non-Consultation: Effects on Foreign Policy-Making in Commonwealth Caribbean States", *International Journal*, Vol. XXIV, 2, Spring 1979.

12. Suggestions for improvement of the uses of expertise are provided by C.J. Lipton, "Government Negotiating Techniques and Strategies", p.8, Centre for Transnational Corporations, UN, New York. An alternative proposal has been made (UNIDO Joint Study on International Industrial Cooperation 1979) to supplement expertise available only in the private market by the formation of a Consultancy Agency, financed on a downward sliding scale by the UN initially, and later through voluntary contributions. To date, nothing has come of this.
An immediate practical consideration might be a directory of specialised consultants in different fields of negotiation; a register which might be updated and verified by relevant intergovernmental agencies. Such directories are already available in the US for domestic purposes.

13. Information in a one-off context must generally be differentiated from the type which is stockable for re-use. Its value when stocked is directly related to local infrastructural capacity for retrieval and use. Information usually has greater value if it is location or case specific rather than centrally stored and transmitted from that point.

14. There is some reason to suspect that the widespread use of multinational computer systems may aggravate the present tensions that exist between nation states and MNCs. It is unlikely, for example, that multinational management information systems could'be made effective without contributing to the homogenization of problem-solving behaviours, cultural values and public attitudes on a worldwide basis. Moreover, multinational computer systems are likely to enhance the power and influence of multinational organisations whose interests transcend national ones: B. Nanus, "Business, Government and the Multinational Computer" *Columbia Journal of World Business*, Spring 1978, p.24.

15. An excellent OECD publication on business information gives a thorough idea of the sources and services of data banks available to private enterprise in industrialised countries. The enormous gap between these types of service and the, as yet, rudimentary organisation of information available to LDC governments, state corporations or private firms is apparent: *New Structures and Strategies for Business Information*, OECD, November 1980.

16. Nanus, *op. cit.* p.21.

INCISIVE DECISIONS
ALAN BENJAMIN

I want to talk about the use of information technology in connection with the Third World, and perhaps make a few controversial statements.

The first is that the opportunities arising from IT for a steady climb towards improved living conditions, health and education, in developing countries are incontestable. Second, these improvements are not really available on any scale without IT. The ability to collect and use data cheaply, to measure performance, to predict, forecast, indicate, and to build economic activity are all assisted uniquely by the use of IT. Strangely enough, these opportunities lie strongest in just those areas of social management which are in the greatest need — health, housing, education, transportation, agricultural research. And IT is an unusually powerful opportunity to reduce the gap between the developed world and the developing world.

The risks, I think we all agree, of widening this gap, are quite frankly the major risks relating to the planet's survival, in any civilised form. They have certainly been well rehearsed and well documented. Notable among them is the mismanagement of information. In some ways this case has been easy to present, because information domination is sensational, publicity-positive, largely surprising and hardly visible. Certainly outside the circles of politically and technologically aware people the topic makes little impact on the developed world, preoccupied as it is with its current economic failure and its changing society.

The power of information is now recognised as a dominant asset. It requires us to have a deep breath, and to haul ourselves over the increasingly high national boundaries to give this problem its rightful attention on a wider basis. People's horizons are generally quite low, until some crisis looms. The 1973 oil war was just such an event. But the urgency and panic of those days has gone from the public mind. It's off the agenda now. But there is a queue of people raising genuine concerns, spectres of disaster, neo-imperialistic postures, as well as sheer mischievousness about IT.

This is a subject where we ought to be crystal clear about motives. They are political, and let us have the courage to name them as such. They are commercial or technological – let us indicate these motives clearly also. Some will argue that it is impossible to separate the different motives and that the developed countries, or at least some of them, benefit from the confusion and the complexity. And indeed if part of the developed world has a deliberately imperialistic goal, then of course this becomes a political argument. So, my case is simply that there is no alternative – a well-known expression in this country at the moment – but for the developing countries to become proficient in IT. And when that occurs, these balances will be gradually restored and the gaps reduced.

Do I hear 'Oh, not another thing in which we have to become self-sufficient'? It may take one or two generations, so getting started is critical. And that's not accurate either: many developing countries *have* started. What is wrong is the priority level given to IT in those countries. It does not rank with the observed desperate needs for water, adequate housing, education and health. It is not obvious to people in the developing countries that all these other high priority areas depend upon IT for their development. And once this priority rises to the top, the benefits will flow.

Much is already being done, though I cannot yet be optimistic. But I can see a framework of effort and objectives which could soon get there. Developing countries do not need to carry the burden of competitive research and development which is currently costing the developed countries an arm and a leg. Nor do they need tomorrow's technology. Nor should they be insulted with yesterday's. Appropriate technology can be a well-maintained second-hand computer – such as many UK schools have – or tomorrow's powerful micro or communications link. It is entirely application dependent. There are many ways in which the use of IT can reap real benefits, and I'll give some examples later. But the incisive decisions needed in developing countries, apart from raising the priority level, is to motivate the application of IT. This is best done by example in each country. Not by demonstrating what is done elsewhere (except as a useful reference) but by doing things experimentally first, and then on the necessary scale. The definition of priority development within countries can soon identify where the application of IT can help. And a major achievement would arise from the creation of a central information access point on the subject.

This is a venture which has eluded all the organisations we have mentioned tonight, and which you might think were capable of doing it; the United Nations, the OECD, and the EEC have singularly failed to do this. Raising the priority level of IT in a developing country means setting up a high-level ministerial focus for IT needs, skills and experience. From this nucleus it would be possible to create a statement of IT policy, highlighting the requirements and interests concerned. These would certainly include education and training, equipment, software and access to information.

But undoubtedly the overriding infrastructure component would be a telecommunications network. Even here, advances with radio transmission, both VHF and through satellites, are leading to independent mobile offices, or IT stations. So the high investments previously contemplated must be, might be, significantly less without too much loss of facility. With new, less expensive, digital exchanges and packaged software, the future cost of a communications infrastructure will become a more manageable investment. In addition, new wind energy developments are opening up the possibilities of decentralised local power supply resources, with costs far below conventional energy power generation.

Now getting access to these facilities is of course a political matter. Relationships between nations shift sometimes dramatically and sometimes quickly. And some basic resources are just not available in some countries. For the supply of these, trading arrangements are vital. But education and training is not an unavailable resource — it is a matter of investment. Increasingly IT and other technologies offer opportunities to reduce such dependencies. The use of IT in education and training offers very exciting speed-up possibilities to the education process in developing countries. The use of teaching systems, teaching programmes, videos, computer-aided instruction, is relatively inexpensive.

The developing countries can perhaps more successfully cooperate in solving the major resource shortage problem. The supply of clean water, agricultural improvements, more effective food production and the planning aspects of major developments in

health care — this co-operation can find its common base in the application of IT to these problems. Centres of development for IT in primary applications, and applications being developed for each primary sector, can share IT resources, adopt reusable software, use common data bases and often take advantage of portable skills. Once the areas of need are highlighted, the transfer of useful technology from developed countries can be more easily searched for — and, I believe, obtained. The example of this kind of arrangement is shown by the function of the UK Council for Computer Development which was formed recently.

But here's another suggestion. Any technology transfer should be accompanied by simultaneous work designed to show how that technology can be indigenised. Any major contract for advice or resources with the developed world should carry an obligation to submit a plan for the transfer of that technology. This would include training trailers, undertaking to maintain a supply of development information, post-installation reviews, basic spares inventories and, say, annual seminars on developments in the application area. This would have to be paid for, but this is relatively low-level outlay which could be invaluable.

I promised examples of how IT can yield benefits to developing countries. The problem is to pick from many, but here are some. They are abbreviated, but all are published. The use of a micro-computer to capture soil crust thickness data and to log air tempera-tures and radiation measurements; result — the decision to invest in irrigation in areas thought agriculturally dead, followed by crop yields which were previously non-existent. An investment simula-tion developed through software, which reduced the costs and improved the output of an agricultural process involving many millions of dollars. The improvements resulted in re-siting the process and increasing the exports by 100%. A study of water salinity in newly-irrigated land by logging digital measurements using a hand-held micro-computer, captured on cassette and then transferred to a mini-computer. The analysis resulted in successful salinity treatment which modified certain crop selling plans; future ground water behaviour in lands still to be reclaimed was modelled on this increased knowledge. One more: the management of an agricultural credit company, controls on mortgages and loans, and assessment of re-advancements. Result — improved cash collec-tion, more predictable cash-flows, more loans, better information for development plans.

And I could go on. There is evidence that useful work carried out suffers, because the developing countries involved do not provide the continuity of staff or training. And that is again a question of priorities. So in the final analysis the benefits of IT are substantial in relation to outlay, which in none of the above cases exceeded a six figure sum. The support programmes from develo-ped countries are insufficiently used in this respect, and that is the fault of the developed countries. New, more understanding atti-tudes are required in the governments of developed countries towards the sensible use of IT as a support measure. Talk to the railway engineer, or the farmer, or the water engineer in a develo-ping country who has seen results — visible, touchable results — from IT. He would be the best reference for its impact. Or talk to a young person in the developing world who has now understood that he can programme, and now comprehends the power in achieving useful goals that skill confers. It's the doing that matters, not the talking. We have a technology, a programmable technology, which is really able to accomodate almost any view of the world we wish to take. It is ours to use for good or bad. The decision is down to us.

Work and/or leisure?

What impact will IT have on the future of work? Will the imperatives of competing in world markets mean that we have any choice
in adopting IT? What jobs will be lost and what gained? What
changes will there be in the type of employment available and what
role should the Trade Unions, business people, educationalists etc.
play in this? Will we have to redefine our notions of leisure? Will
there be a case for a minimum income regardless of employment to
allow an individual to combine more traditional types of work with
activities which are socially desirable but at present voluntary or
lowly paid?

**Chairman: Professor Howard Rosenbrock. Speakers: Jonathan
Gershuny, Clive Jenkins, Mike Cooley, David Fairbairn.**

GUESSTIMATIONS

Apart from the threat to privacy, the effect of IT on employment
must by now be the most thoroughly discussed area of this whole
subject. Yet it is evident, from the contributions to this section, that
we are still in a state of lamentable ignorance about it. Here, for
instance, is Clive Jenkins, in effect saying 'Brothers, you've seen
nothing yet', and predicting the most dire consequences still to
come. In his paper, that is not much more than an assertion; but
Mike Cooley, in his very thorough essay, supports it with massive
(though necessarily selective) facts and figures.

But then, here also is Jonathan Gershuny, admittedly an optimist, using a closely-reasoned analysis of the 'informal economy' to
reach just the opposite conclusion — namely that IT can lead to
renewed growth, if only we have enough faith in it to take the risk of
installing the necessary infrastructure, on Keynesian principles.
And David Fairbairn takes a similar line, even though he describes
himself as a pessimist.

Plainly, there is so far nothing like enough evidence for anyone
to be able to do more than make guesses, informed by little more
than their gut feelings, and supported only by a modicum of extra-
polation from some past experience — most of which is not compar-
able enough to found any reliable predictions, even if one were
entitled to assume that what has happened in the past will always
happen in the same way in the future.

Skills and esteem

So we are left no wiser about whether there will be more jobs, or fewer. But there are some important predictions about the *kinds* of jobs there will be. Cooley, for instance, mentions the de-skilling effect which IT might have — a subject to which he has already made a notable contribution, with Howard Rosenbrock and others, in the Council for Science and Society's important report on *New Technology: Society, Employment and Skill*.

No one, at least in these papers, seems to have discussed the consequences of unemployment on the unemployed themselves. These are quite different today from what they used to be. One tends to forget that the curse of unemployment cannot be mitigated by money alone. In the Great Depression of the 1930s, the unemployed suffered appalling deprivations; that was found to be intolerable, and today's unemployed are therefore supported by the Welfare State at a *material* standard of living often very little lower than if they were in work. But that still leaves them with a pervasive sense of futility and rejection: their skills are unwanted and unused, they are contributing nothing, and they are deprived of the esteem of their community on which their own self-esteem in turn depends. Our society still largely values people for the work they contribute to it, rather than for what they are. We ask 'What are you?' rather than 'Who are you?'. As long as that remains so, increased leisure will be a curse rather than a blessing. What seems to be at fault here is not just the economic system, but more particularly the social esteem structure. Besides, *must* we all measure our own worth by the values that others place on us? Are their judgments likely to be any better than our own? Can we not have enough confidence in ourselves to make ourselves independent of the valuations of others?

Economics and its mysteries

Back in the area of economics, David Fairbairn's major point is simple, but unanswerable. I have a special sympathy with it, for I remember asking just such naive questions when I was a child in the 1930s. Here were millions only too ready to work. Heaven knew there was plenty of work that cried out to be done. Why couldn't they be allowed to do it? Because there wasn't enough demand for the goods they could produce, I was told. But surely, I argued, *they* wanted more goods? Yes, but they couldn't afford them. Quite so, said I — but surely that was only because they weren't being paid any wages to buy them with?

Then and now, I have never been given any answers to those questions that I have found even remotely convincing. All over the world, there is work of all kinds to be done — much of it satisfying, rewarding, and useful. All over the world, people are willing to do that work and they and others need — indeed often long for — the goods and services it could produce. And yet, with all our ingenuity, resourcefulness and even goodwill, we still do not seem to have found any way of breaking the mysterious logjam that seems to stop it all from happening. So far as I can make out, the logs have names like 'balance of payments', 'inflation', 'prime rate', 'money supply', 'terms of trade', and other such abstractions which no one has ever been able to explain to me — or, I suspect, to a good many other people.

Resistance to change

Perhaps I have a blind spot about theoretical economics. Or perhaps — as I would prefer to believe — this is baboon language, beyond the understanding of mere chimpanzees. But Fairbairn has a different explanation: he puts it all down to limits on the rates at which we can change things. May be so, but why do we have to be so resistant to change? As a would-be law reformer, I have long since learnt that to get even the most obvious and desirable changes made in the laws of the UK requires the patience of Job and the persistence of a fox-terrier. Seven years from idea to implementation is positively quick: most reforms take much longer. That is why, here, this is not a job for the young — they lose patience too quickly.

Not so, mind you, in most other countries: when they see a good idea, they get on with adopting it. New Zealand leads the Commonwealth in law reform; Japan leads the world in industrial innovation; West Germany leads the West in industrial relations — through a system devised for it by British trade unionists after the last war, but still not adopted here because of intractable union opposition.

No, this extreme resistance to change is a peculiarly British phenomenon. For instance, every country in the world has a class system; but we are now the only industrialised one left whose class indicators are not earning power, skill, responsibility, education, culture, or even grammar and syntax — but, of all unbelievable things, still the old feudal indicators of accents and meal-times. Where else in the developed world does one half of the population have its dinner at noon and its tea at 6, while the other half has its lunch at 1 and its dinner at 8? And where else is the first half still paid by the week and the second by the month, so perpetuating a stultifying 'dissonance of time horizons' between the short-sighted and the far-sighted?

Britain is of course unique — thanks to the English Channel — in having 916 years of continuous history, uninterrupted by lost wars, foreign occupations, or even major civil wars or bloody revolutions. Every other European country has found itself more than once looking at the smoking ruins of its previous civilisation, and having to roll up its shirtsleeves to start again from scratch – often in the lifetimes of people who still remember the last cataclysm before that one. This gives them great scope for radical reform. One can only hope that we do not have to go through the agony of a similar historical discontinuity before we can finally get rid of some of the more paralysing millstones that we still have clanking round our collective neck.

Paul Sieghart

GROWTH, TECHNOLOGY AND THE INFORMAL ECONOMY
JONATHAN GERSHUNY

In looking at the effects new technology will have on our lives, we have to make distintion between two different sorts of change. The first is what economists call "process innovation" – the use of new technologies to make existing products more efficiently. The second is "product innovation" – the development of new markets, finding new goods and new sorts of services to sell to households.

This second sort of change is much more difficult to think about than the first; after all, the new markets are by definition not here yet, and it is all too easy to dismiss speculation about them as merely science fiction. So let us start with process innovation (which, in any case, may well be the more important of the two).

We have got a given set of commodities, a given set of goods and services, which have established markets; the new technology permits us to produce them more cheaply, using less labour per unit of output. That is the effect of the microprocessor chip, for instance. We use the chip to make industrial robots and in turn we use the robots to make our washing machines or whatever and at the same time we use microprocessors to simplify the design of those washing machines. The effect is to vastly increase the labour productivity – and we can do this across a very wide range of manufacturing industry.

Similar effects are found throughout a large part of service industries. Computers, mark-reading devices and cheap electronic storage media can displace a substantial part of the clerical, money-handling, information-giving sorts of activities.

These changes don't lead to very much new economic activity. They lead to a displacement of labour but they do not lead to new markets. In principle they could lead to an increase in the size of existing markets, however. The reduction in prices that results from process innovation could induce more people to buy more of particular existing products, and if it did that it would raise the overall level of economic activity. But what if the markets for each of the products we are currently consuming were effectively saturated? It is widely believed that we are in something like this situation at present. Virtually all households have televisions and washing machines. Most household that could run a car already have one, and the newer consumer foods like the video-cassette recorders seem to be produced so efficiently that they don't require much employment to make them. Similar restraints are found in the service industries. No one believes that increased efficiency at supermarket check-outs is going to product more demand for those sorts of services.

To put it baldly, the threat of the chip comes down to this: it seems to increase the efficiency in production without leading to a compensating increase in demand. Overall, it may lead to a depression in the level of economic activity. If this dismal view were not sufficiently worrying, we also have to bear in mind the current prospects for public employment.

In the 1950s and 1960s, a considerable part of the growth in developed economies was in publicly provided services, particularly education and medicine. It now seems that this growth, too, has stopped — perhaps because people believe that this sort of expenditure is inefficiently used or administered, or perhaps because there are ideological objections to public expenditure. But whatever the reason, few people really now believe that economic growth can be restarted by increasing public employment.

To set against this pessimistic view we seem to have only the rather problematical prospects of future product innovations. Can we think of a new product, new sorts of markets, that might be sufficient to generate a growth, a new growth, and a restart in economic activity? The answer relies not so much on an economic argument as a socialogical one. It relies upon a rather unfamiliar piece of social history, a rather unfamiliar argument concerning the so-called "informal economy".

Consider the two decades following the Second World War. They saw a very wide range of different social changes which included one with really major implications in the organisation of our economy. This was the process of change in the way households acquired their services. During the 1950s and 1960s households in Britain in general had a very substantial increase in the range of services they could consume. Their standard of domestic comfort, their access to transport, the accessibility of entertainment all improved for most households almost beyond recognition. Particularly for the poorer two-thirds of the population, the end of the 1960s saw a style of life that was in most material aspects vastly preferable to that of say the mid-1930s.

But this improvement in the accessibility of services did not come because people were buying more services. And the improvement in the level of domestic comfort did not come about because households employed more servants. It came about because they purchased household equipment and produced domestic services themselves. Households increased their mobility, not by buying more trips on buses or trains but by buying cars and driving them themselves. The accessibility of entertainment was increased, not by going more frequently to the cinema or theatre but by buying televisions.

Developments of this sort were arguably the most important social changes to take place in those decades, involving a process of industrialisation of services which is quite similar to the nineteenth century processes of industrialisation and division of labour in manufacturing industries. There is the same process of capitalisation (in most cases investment in machinery like washing machines and fridges and televisions and motor cars), the difference being that this machinery was stored in households and not in factories. There is the same process of embodiment oif skills, though in this case not so much in machinery as in what we might think of as software to be used in conjunction with machinery — gramophone records for example.

The most important thing about such developments is their effect upon the money economy. The industrialisation of services generated a very wide range of new sorts of demands for new products. It led to the growth of new markets for consumer durables, consumer electronics, "white goods", motor cars and the materials and the services associated with all those goods. The new markets were for products which enabled the provision of new services within the household, the provision of new services within the "informal economy".

Now suppose you were asked what sorts of production, what sorts of industry, lay at the heart of the post-war years of economic growth and prosperity. Which industrial sectors would you choose? Odds-on you would go for consumer goods, vehicle manufacturing and so on — exactly the industries producing for the markets generated by this industrialisation of services. That is because of the connection between the informal economy and formal economic growth. The new markets for the products of the formal money economy go to feed the parallel production activities which proceed on an unpaid basis in the informal economy. The growth of production of services in the informal economy provides the markets for the products of the formal economy. In the post-war decades it was the growth of informal production of domestic services, transport services and entertainment that provided the basis for the markets of washing machines, televisions and motor cars which in turn provided the mainspring of growth in the formal economy.

That is a piece of unconventional economic history. Now let us return to the question: what sorts of product innovation can generate economic growth in the future? The historical argument outlined above does suggest some sort of an answer. Just as in the 1950s and 1960s you might look into the future to the development of new markets which aid the informal production of new sorts of services, the likely products now are those which use the new information technologies to enable households to produce new sorts of services in the informal manner. The informal provision of services here would rely on a number of different sorts of product from the formal economy. It would rely, obviously, on the microprocessors and the information storage devices like video cassette recorders which will be installed in households. It would also require a new information transmission network in some ways similar to the conventional telephone system but in one crucial way quite different. The information-carrying capacity of the wires would have to be very much greater. To give an idea of the problems an ordinary domestic telephone line would take something like thirty seconds to build just one complete frame of television picture. So simply transmitting continuous television pictures needs an information-carrying capacity of about 1,000 conventional telephone lines.

Here are some examples of the new sorts of services which might become available as a result of the new products and the new sorts of information industry. In the sphere of domestic services we can construct systems for automatic, centralised monitoring and control of the range of household functions like heating, lighting and safety (and these household systems can themselves be linked to local security and safety services). In addition we might imagine information packages giving advice on household operations, on personal problems, or perhaps reminding us about household maintenance tasks.

In entertainment, we already have home box office systems giving households the options of access by cables to a much more varies range of entertainment material that can be provided on a mass broadcasting basis. By a simple extension we could imagine a subscription scheme which would use such systems to promote new films and musical performances which otherwise would not find a market, either in theatres or in broadcasting.

In the transport-communications area, the same infrastructure and the same domestic equipment would allow armchair shopping, and the transfer of money electronically. There would presumably be video telephones and other sophistications, such as computerised switching to permit conversations not just with one specified individual but with anyone who wanted to talk about some specific topic.

In education, we can imagine the proliferation of packages for remote education training – not just Open University programmes, but a vast range of specialist material could be transmitted in this way.

Medicine: we could provide continuous care at home through remote monitoring of chronic disorders. Similarly we could develop packages for remote diagnosis, and certainly we could have packages for remote interactive counselling for medical and other sorts of problems.

When we consider each of these innovations individually, the costs – particularly the infrastructure costs – appear prohibitively high (though some, particularly the entertainment examples, might

well turn out to be viable in isolation). In general we could not justify a "wired city" infrastructure on the basis of, say, potential educational innovations. But if the infrastructure costs of a number of these services were shared, their economics would become much more plausible. Once the infrastructure is built, marginal costs of most of these examples amount to little more than the software that they require. It does appear that the same basic infrastructure could be designed to serve all the examples listed here, and there are probably many more sorts of services that could be provided.

The markets which would develop in this way would not be just for hardware and infrastructure. A new category of products of great importance would be software. Consumption of software has not been very substantial in the past. The only sort of final consumption that really falls into this category is television and radio programmes, and recorded music. But this may be a crucially important and perhaps, in growth terms, the dominant commodity in the economic growth of the 1990s.

The industrialisation of services has already had a substantial effect on the nature of commodities produced by some sorts of work. Consider, for example, actors or musicians. They used to stand on stages and produce performances for an audience that was physically present. Once the performance was finished their product and the service they produced was completely used up. To entertain more people they had to perform again. Now, once they are filmed or recorded they produce not a final product, not a final service which is instantaneously consumed, but rather a piece of software which is combined subsequently and elsewhere to provide a final service again and again if it is desired, for as many people as have the appropriate hardware.

The question is: is this process necessarily labour-displacing? Certainly it means that each individual's performance requires a smaller input from the artist. But equally, each performance is very much cheaper — so very many people can afford to experience it. The reduction in price due to the industrialisation of production of the service vastly increases the potential market. The net effect has been that the number of professional musicians, for example, has increased very substantially over the last few decades.

Future social innovations of this kind will depend heavily on software in the broadest sense of the term. Actors and musicians now produce largely in the form of software and if the sorts of innovation described above do take place, so too will the doctors, and teachers and shopkeepers and firemen who design algorithms or record video programmes which go ultimately to provide new services to household. And we can at least hope that the same sorts of employment prospects will follow. We can hope that the increased efficiency of production and the higher quality of provision will generate large enough new markets to increase employment in these areas. So we can see a wide range of new markets: markets for fibre optics and other cable, switching equipment, communications satellites for the infrastructure, hardware for the home, maintenance and installation services and, most important, new software products providing for the enormously wide range of potential applications of the new technology to the informal production of services.

So this is the argument in a nutshell. We use communications infrastructure and other sorts of commodities to produce new sorts of services outside the money economy. In effect the informal economy is the source of demand for products of the formal economy. If we can devise new forms of informal production we may thereby generate new markets, new employment, new economic activity. This paper has only scratched the surface of the discussion.

Perhaps it all sounds a little unconvincing, a shade too close to science fiction. But put yourself in the position of someone in, say, 1930. What prospects would you have seen then? Specifically what would have been your reaction to economists who actually somehow foresaw the pattern of development through the 1950s? There are two likely sorts of reaction. The first is an inward-turning, pessimistic reaction which sees no positive prospects at all. Because it cannot see any hope for improvement it turns — as happend in the 1930s — to increasingly authoritarian political regimes to contain the rising levels of discontent, or perhaps to foreign policy adventurism to distract it.

The second reaction, by contrast, is optimistic, along the lines of the New Dealers in the USA. They foresaw prospects for economic growth in the future, even though the precise shape of the new markets to them in 1930 was obscure. They were reasonably certain that the new markets of the future would rely on certain sorts of physical infrastructure, like roads and electricity supply, so they built dams, roads and electricity grids. Now this provided direct employment in the short term at the very least, but they also thought it quite likely that this sort of investment might encourage more growth in the more distant future. Indeed it did turn out that precisely the infrastructure developed in the New Deal was the necessary basis for the growth of the markets of the 1950s and 1960s. Those new markets for washing machines, refrigerators, cars and so on were in effect made possible by the infrastructure investment in the electricity grids and the roads in the 1930s.

I suspect that we are now in a position similar to that of the 1930s. Now as then — and to a degree not experienced certainly since the Second World War — the future prospects for our developed economies are obscure to us. Whatever we do now will be a leap in the dark. But we have nothing to lose by following the New Deal route, investing in "wired city" infrastructure, building facilities for communal services, retraining our workforces to use the new technologies. At the very least we create direct employment by doing so. And the science fiction may turn out to be 1990s fact. The one thing we can be absolutely sure of is that if we don't make these investments now, we won't have the growth in the 1990s.

ACCELERATING DAMAGE
CLIVE JENKINS

What has happened in the last three years is of critical importance, not technologically but politically. We have a quite insane radical-right government and the problem is that it is in control of one of the great money markets of the world. And to our great distress and damage we have had a government returned in the United States which resembles this, controlling the other great money market of the world. So we have a convergence of the East Coast money market and the City of London and thus we have a man-made depression.

As a result, we have accelerated the damage that we being done to the classic old manufacturing sectors — chemicals, engineering, transportation and commercial services outside the fields of health, education and person-to-person care.

What is still not appreciated by the British is that the very well-managed economies of the Far East — often militaristic and very well-controlled indeed — have already leapfrogged over all of us. Not only us and the Americans, but the Belgians and the French and the Dutch and the Germans. You may take the adversarial, confrontationist view that we have to catch up with them and we have to leapfrog over them. But that is, philosophically, fundamentally wrong and even absurd.

Aneurin Bevan said in 1955 that the United Kingdom's islands were made of solid coal surrounded by fish; and his criticism was that the government of the day had created a shortage of both. I shall update that statement: these islands are of solid coal (the EEC has finished our fish) floating on a bubble of oil and gas. This is the only industrialised nation in the world, albeit with a stock of aged equipment, which is more than self-sufficient in every kind of energy apart from hydro-electric power. In the last five years we have discovered the three richest coalfields in our history. Rich and cheap. And we have been mining coal since before the Roman centurians led their legions on to our shores. There are clearly enormous reserves — decades of gas — beneath our coalfields, and therefore we have a unique opportunity.

At the moment we are spending our oil and gas revenues to keep people out of work because this government believes that market forces have a special quality, a quality of morality and excellence. Since September 1981, every major manufacturing company which had held on to skilled draughtsmen, supervisors, technicians, managers, has started sacking them or not replacing them. No employer now believes there is a light at the end of the tunnel — unless that light is a train coming towards him.

The true unemployment figure is now 4.3 million, including the people on special schemes; and if the Conservatives run their full term it will be 5 million. We are never going back to full employment. The real problem is how we cope if we have a Labour government and it creates 2 million jobs in three years as it is planning to do. That will still leave us with a job shortage of 3 million. Our other difficulty is that there are a million people at the moment who have not worked for a year, and this year we are going to have 900,000 young people coming out of full-time education who have nowhere to go.

That's the good news, because technology has not even started decimating jobs yet. But if you are employed, working with information on paper, you ought to be on the World Wildlife Fund's list of endangered species. In the City of London, that is in insurance, banking, commercial services, shipping brokerage, commodity trading, in the next two years at the most, 350,000 jobs are going. And that is just the first tranche. Most of those will not be trade unionists; they are not protected and they will be decimated.

So what can we do to adjust to this? We should use the railways as the growth point, because electrifying the railways will generate ripples outwards. We will need more power stations, more steel, metering equipment. And we can have a fibre optics network alongside the railway lines. That is the best place to start. That, in turn, will provide other jobs in people-to-people industries, in health and education, and making sure that old people do not die behind closed doors because no one is watching and caring.

The difficulty is that training people, assessing people, interviewing people takes time and all the civil engineering and reconstruction programmes will be bottlenecked because we have not got enough craftsmen, enough professional engineers, enough managers, enough physicists, enough surveyors.

New technology has cost very few jobs so far. But it will not provide any trade-off either; there will be no substantial numbers of new jobs created by it anywhere. What we can do, however, is use it for welfare to create jobs in renewing the infrastructure of our society.

But it is worrying because the situation is now getting out of control and this government has not idea of the consequences of what it is doing. A different government can make sure that we put resources into basic infrastructure renewal, and we will have to employ new technology to give us the money to do that. We shall

have to mobilise the pension funds. There is more liquid cash per capita available in this country that in any other in the world. So we will mobilise. We will have new banks, new entrepreneurial management agencies, and we will go and look for opportunities.

I only hope we are not too late. Enormous damage has been done. It has not got anything to do with new technology, but until we harness new technology, new technology is going to harm us further.

COMPUTERS, POLITICS AND UNEMPLOYMENT
MIKE COOLEY

There is a widespread belief that technological change, as represented by automation, computerisation and the use of robotic systems, will free human being from soul destroying, routine tasks and leave them free to engage in more creative, fulfilling activities[1]. It is further suggested that this will inevitably lead to a shorter working week, longer holidays and more leisure time. Viewed thus, these technologies are perceived to be liberatory and positive, and are seen as the transmission lines along which will flow an ever increasing 'quality of life'.

I shall try to show that such a socio-technical scenario is at best premature and simplistic, or at worst, a deliberate attempt by industrialists and politicians to placate the well founded fears of the community at large about the wider social multiplier effects of these new technologies in general and their impact on employment in particular.

To review what these implications might be, it is necessary to view the computer and these new technologies as part of a technological continuum which started some 400 years ago. Computerised equipment, however sophisticated, is nonetheless, at base, a *means of production*. As such, it brings in its wake liberatory potential on the one hand, but on the other hand, the contradictions and conflicts which have always accompanied changes in the means of production at earlier historical stages. It would be a serious mistake to view the computer as an isolated phenomenon. It should be considered within the context of the political, economic and ideological assumptions of the society which has given rise to it. It is true to say that technological change within the 'advanced societies' has occurred within a framework described by the rule of the three Rs: Rationalisation, Reorganisation and Redundancy. It seems desirable, therefore, to view the impact on employment in an interactive form, and look at the consequences at the following three discernible levels.

Impact on Employment

It has long been recognised that it is extremely difficult to separate that component of redundancy which can be attributed directly to either automation or computerisation[2]. Thus there is as yet no universal agreement as to the employment impact of computers and micro-electronics. A number of somewhat optimistic Government Reports suggest that job creation schemes may be able to match job reductions[3]. Some academic researchers on the other hand suggest that a mere 10% of the present labour force will be capable of providing all the material needs of British society within 30 years[4].

Albert Booth, the Minister of Employment in the last Labour Government, is quoted as saying that the introduction of micro-processors should increase productivity which in turn will increase employment through investment in new manufacturing areas. Quite the reverse point of view is taken by Clive Jenkins who says, 'full employment talk is an absurdity'[5].

An examination of some specific areas strongly indicates that Clive Jenkins is right and Albert Booth is wrong. The NORG report for the French Government calculates that modern computing technology in banks over the next ten years will reduce the staff in this area by 30%. Similar figures apply to the insurance industry. It also suggests as far as general office environment is concerned, that many of France's secretaries and typists could be replaced by word processing systems[6]. Similarly, a recent estimate by Siemens suggests that by 1990 40% of the present office work (in West Germany) could be carried out by computerised systems. The West German trade unions have translated this into figures and have calculated that it would mean a staggering loss of 2 million of West Germany's 5 million secretarial and typing jobs. In the United Kingdom, ASTMS have forecast that 2.6 million information workers will lose their jobs by 1985, and by 1991 the figure will have risen to 3.9 million.

The significance of the impact in this area may be judged when one compares the United States' 400,000 word processors with 45,000 in West Germany and 9,000 in the United Kingdon as at June 1978. It has been suggested by Logica that one typist on a word processor can do the work of 4.5 to 5 typists on traditional type-writers. The impact that these, and computerisation in general, will have on 'traditional women's jobs' and the form and nature of the jobs that remain have been described in detail in a recent paper[7].

One would be quite mistaken to believe that these problems of unemployment lie in some far distant future, thereby providing a time scale in which concerned politicians, liberal employers and perceptive trade unions will identify the problems and take remedial action. The problems are with us here and now.

Nor are these structural changes limited to 'lower level' clerical activities. In the fields of draughtsmanship and design, the introduction of computer-based systems can result in staff requirements of one eleventh or, more typically, one eighth of those previously employed[8]. The consequences can therefore be regarded as spreading right across the entire field of white collar work from routine clerical tasks, on the one hand, right through the occupational spectrum to high level, creative, intellectual work.

The above is precisely what happened at earlier historical stages when manual work was subjected to technological change. Some trade union researchers now take the view that this will result in up to four or five million unemployed in the United Kingdom by 1990[9]. Should these levels of unemployment materialise, the political implications will be truly enormous. The impact is most likely to be experienced by the young and 'the old' (it will be shown elsewhere the 'old' in this context can mean 30 to 40).

Geoffrey Holland, director of special programmes at the Manpower Services Commission, has recently expressed concern that many unskilled young people may never get a job and therefore drift outside society without any union to represent their interests. This group, he says, could pose major social and political problems: 'Time is not on our side, and we must find ways of securing access to some form of work for these young people even if it's in the 'unpaid' public work.'[10]

The prospect of large-scale structural uneployment has caused Sir Charles Carter, the Chairman of the Research and Management Committee of the Social Studies Institute in London, to predict that it could lead to collapse of the present political system[11]. In spite of these widespread concerns, there is as yet, apart from the Government's trivial and irrelevant 'Job Creation Schemes', no indication that at nation-state level an infrastructure is being set up to deal with these problems. The position of the Government in the United Kingdom seems to be that if society embraces these new technologies with open arms, there will in any case be no problem of unemployment. There are now fears that the Government is deliberately interfering with reports on the consequences of these new technologies. For example, the three white collar unions concerned have accused the Government of putting pressure on the 'Think Tank' to produce an optimistic report. The response of ASTMS to this was: The Report is whitewash. The Think Tank has come up with a bland document which bears no relation to the facts'.

Some trade unionists now take the view that the Government and the large corporations are deliberately misleading the public as to the employment consequences of these new technologies. Further, they point out that at a time when sociologists and others predict growing unrest, particularly amongst the young as they are denied the right to work, the state is gradually building up repressive forces of containment. This tends to be reflected at local level, where in the North West, Conservatives are calling for harsher sentences and corporal punishment for 'delinquency' at a time when the social conditions created by the technology they so actively advocate, inevitably lead to such social reactions. These developments indicate repressive 'law and order' methods of handling effects rather than the political honesty of facing up to some of the fundamental causes.

At a less sinister level, there seems to be the belief in some political circles that the employment crisis will be merely a temporary one, and that the levels of unemployment we are now experiencing are cyclical rather than structural. It is also pointed out optimistically that technological change at earlier historical stages did not result in dramatic desplacements of the workforce. Such a view fails to recognise the scale, nature and rate of technological change with which we are involved. This can best be understood if we view what is happening in some kind of historical perspective. Figure 1 shows the composition of the workforce in the United States since the beginning of the 1880s. It will be seen that at that time some 80% of the workforce was engaged in agriculture. This activity was gradually subjected to mechanisation, the use of chemicals and finally, phases of automation such that approximately 6% of the workforce now produces an agricultural produce several times as great as the 80% were able to produce at the beginning of the 1800s.

In the course of this development, those displaced from agriculture increasingly moved into manufaturing. This too was subjected to mechanisation and automation, and eventually, the rate of technological change overcame the rate of expansion, and this activity also began to contract from the late 1950s and early 1960s and is now down to perhaps 35% of the population. During the same period, the white collar administrative scientific management area was growing. This is now also subjected to massive technological change; and structural unemployment is now evident within this area as well.

It is worth recalling that it took hundreds of years to evolve agriculture, yet the scale and nature of its labour content was transformed in a mere 180 years. Manufacturing industry in its present forms may be said to be approximately 200 years old. It was developed and transformed in this very short length of time. The white collar administrative areas will be transformed in an even shorter length of time. What we are witnessing, when viewed historically, is a change in the organic composition of capital as processes are rendered capital intensive rather than labour intensive.

One of the central objectives of the form of science and technology within Western society (and one includes here the so-called socialist countries) has been to replace living labour, in both its manual and intellectual forms, with dead labour or fixed capital. Even over the past fifteen years, the consequences of the rate and nature of these changes is evident (see Figures 2 and 3). Society may well have reached a stage at which the rate of change is now beginning to be counter productive; those concerned with energy and material conservation would certainly suggest so in a different context, and societies may now have to consider how they can apply laterally the technical and scientific ability we have acquired, rather than pursue the linear drive forward which now characterises the technologically advanced nations.

Shortfall of Staff

The shortfall of *computer workers* would appear to contradict the general thesis that this form of technological change will give rise to structural unemployment. It has been suggested that during 1977 this shortfall was approximately 25%, and that at the beginning of 1979 it was probably approaching 35%[12].

There would appear to be a number of related reasons for this. The first of these might be described as a 'transitional misfit'. This is the gap which exists between the rate at which new systems and installations are being introduced, and the availability of staff to handle them. The rate of introduction is itself related to the dramatic reductions in hardware prices and the cost of facilities to house them Even computer specialists themselves find it difficult to conceptualise the speed of this development. A car production analogy will dramatically illustrate the point. If the automotive industry had developed as fast as the computer industry, it would now be possible to buy a Rolls Royce for £1.45. This would be capable of doing three million miles to the gallon, and you could put five of them on the tip of your little finger! The lack of planning for this exponential rate of change is in part the problem, but there are others.

The rate of technological change brings in its wake an ever

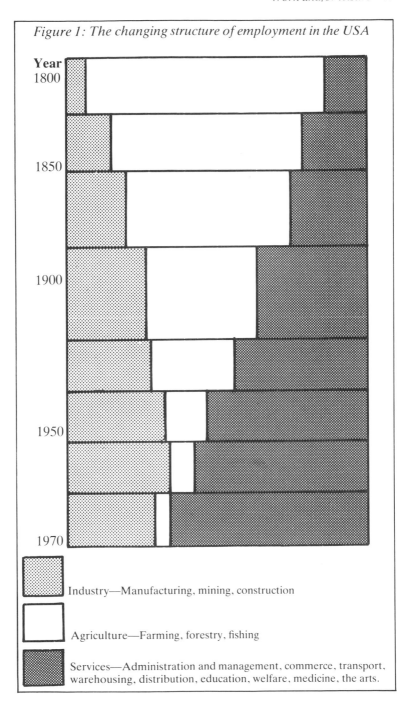

Figure 1: The changing structure of employment in the USA

Industry—Manufacturing, mining, construction

Agriculture—Farming, forestry, fishing

Services—Administration and management, commerce, transport, warehousing, distribution, education, welfare, medicine, the arts.

Figure 2: Telephone exchange-relative sizes and labour ratios needed to make them

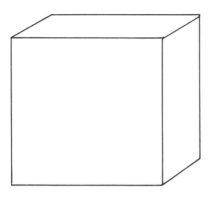

TXE4 first generation electronic

Electromechanical Strowger

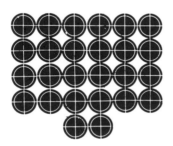

26 Workers

10 Workers

System X 1990 fully electronic

1 Worker

increasing rate of obsolescence of equipment and systems; the ever decreasing lifespan of fixed capital. This is accompanied by an ever increasing obsolescence of 'scientific knowledge'. So dramatic is this that it has been asserted that if one could divide knowledge into its quartiles of outdatedness, all those over the age of 40 would find themselves the same quartile as Pythagoras and Archimedes!

This development finds its most frenzied form in the field of 'computerisation'. Mr. Norman McRay, deputy editor of the *Economist* stated as far back as January 1972: The speed of technological advance has been so tremendous during the last decade, that the useful life of the knowledge of many of those trained to use computers has been about three years'. Because they view their workforce in narrow and exploitative terms, employers invariably seek to find an employee with narrow, specialised skills, (a dedicated appendage for a dedicated system!). Those narrowly specialised in the use of ICL 1900s are thus a dying breed and there will be fewer and fewer jobs for George 3 experts. Those introducing 2900 systems will want a fresh-faced graduate specialist, whereas the older person experienced on George 3 will be displaced. This problem arises from the overspecialisation of training (the word 'training' is appropriate as distinct from 'education') and can now be regarded as counter productive. What is necessary is the following:
1 A much more univeral form education to provide for a knowledge base sufficiently wide and extensive to permit the computer specialist to move from one field to another.
2 A sympathetic training programme for those already in industry who lack knowledge of the new systems being introduced.

A further problem is that modern industry is so highly synchronised and 'efficient' that there is no room for human beings to experiment or to learn, Most companies are therefore reluctant to take in 'trainees' and even those who have pursued a specialist course elsewhere still find enormous difficulty in obtaining their first job. In additon to this, there is the growing hostility amongst able and sensitive young people to the objectives, policies and practices of large-scale manufacturing industries, vast commercial organisations, and Government bureaucracies.

This growing reaction should not be viewed as a peculiarly British phenomenon. Students in Germany, France, Italy and the United States, all display similar attitudes. For example, students in the United States included the following as 'bad words' about our present day society: 'professional, system, organisation, management, cost-effectiveness, statistical controls, programming, calculation'[13]. In addition, some 76% of the sample thought that there should be less emphasis on money and more emphasis on self-

IT MAKES IT SO MUCH EASIER TYPING OUT THE REDUNDANCY NOTICES

expression in our lives. Yet the whole way in which computer work is taught is to deny human beings any form of self-expression and reduce them to an appendage of the machine. Young people's rejection therefore, of those 'training schemes' which will provide them with 'a skill' to do one narrow kind of computer work for a short length of time (and then to face the occupational scrapheap!) are far more significant than our politicians and economic and scientific planners seem to understand.

Societal Costs

Computers, we are invariably told, are introduced to increase the efficiency of the organisations which use them This very narrow accountants' concept of efficiency is based on the input and output of an individual organisation and takes no account at all of the wider societal costs of such 'efficiency'. As shown above, these systems invariably displace labour. Whilst this may make a multinational company look efficient, the nation state in which it operates then has to pick up the bill for the cost of those who are unemployed. It will be seen from Figure 4 that to maintain an unemployed worked with two children in the United Kingdom can cost as much as 105% of the average industrial wage in the short-term and 90% in the long-term. An important report on these matters suggests that each nation state will have to look very carefully at the cost to society as a whole which flows from the apparent optimisation of resources in individual organisations*[14].

We shall, therefore, see growing contradictions in these concepts of efficiency. On the one hand, management consultants and systems designers will seek to optimise and maximise the human/computer interface in individual organisation when the direct consequences of this will be growing structural unemployment at large. Secondly, attempts will be made to utilise the equipment and systems to the full at a time when society at large will increasingly demand a shorter working week, longer holidays, more leisure time and more work sharing and rotations of functions. All of these, it should be noted, are perceived by management consultants to be elements of inefficiency.

The costs of unemployment indicated above are merely the first level economic costs. Much more difficult to quantify are the wider social multiplier effects, such as the degradation of unemployment, the neurosis, the drug taking, the illness, the inter-personal violence and the decline of inner city areas. None of our present accountancy systems take any of these into consideration and it is clear that a new political framework will have to be found in which these can be measured and taken fully into account in our planning procedures.

These considerations will correctly be constraints on the rate at which individual organisations introduce these new technologies: for the societal effects are far too great to be left in the hands of the GECs, Plesseys and IBMs of this world. Profit maximisation in individual enterprises will increasingly be found to be an unacceptable criterion on which to judge the desirability or otherwise of introducing systems of this kind. This in turn will have profound effects on our economic, policital and social thinking.

Some industrialists and politicians argue that we may have to accept the development of a 'dual economy' with the so-called productive and non-productive sectors. There would, however, appear to be very real political dangers in this. It could mean that as processes become capital intensive rather than labour intensive those large sectors of the population who are displaced would be left to engage in therapeutic, 'do-it-yourself' activities at a community or service level with no real political or economic power in the traditional sense[16]. This could result in the restructuring of industry such that the large corporations employed a small elite who would enjoy advantages denied the rest of the community such as company cars, international travel and medical care. Even if their 'life expectancy' in these large corporations is short, it is conceivable that their critical faculties and social concerns would be silenced by this form of economic anaesthetic. They may therefore be willing to

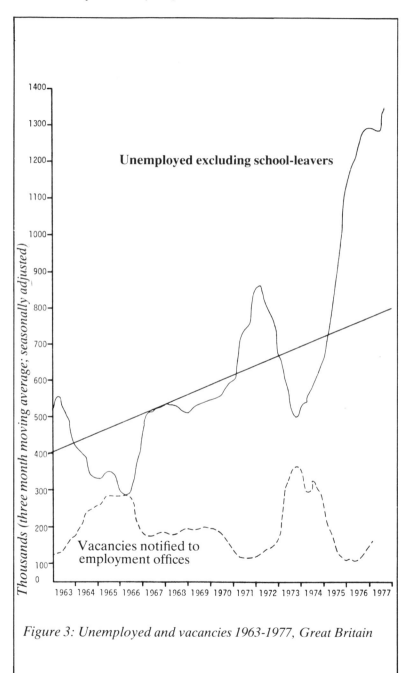

Figure 3: Unemployed and vacancies 1963-1977, Great Britain

share in the ethos of these large corporations and conspire against the public at large, in a form of grandiose 'I'm all right Jack' attitude.

This in turn could lead to a new form of industrial feudalism in which the large multinational corporations would determine both the way in which science and technology develop, and even the educational structures necessary to meet its requirements.

The Trade Union response to these problems has as yet been slow and indecisive. This is in part due to a lingering technological optimism in which it is believed that we can have an ever-increasing rate of production and consumption which tends to ignore energy and material constraints. There are, however, growing signs of an awareness that the present levels of unemployment are not going to decline and are likely to increase dramatically.

The Trade Union responses to these are various. At a general level we will see increasing demands for a shorter working week, longer holidays and more leisure time. It is significant in this context that the first strike in the German steel industry for 50 years is centring on this issue[17].

In Italy, the Metalworkers' Union has negotiated a remarkable agreement which provides for 150 hours 'sabbatical' every year for each of its metalworkers. During this time they are free to study any subject of their own choice as part of a work sharing scheme. This form of development is extremely important, because it implies that if we are to have a dual economy, each human being shall have the right to be active in both sectors. Politically, this is of great importance since it will mean that human beings can play their dual role in society, as both producers and consumers.

The lucky ones

It is sometimes assumed by those who lose their jobs due to technological change, that those who remain are 'the lucky ones'. Such a view fails to recognise that frequently the assumptions which on the one hand displace large groups of workers also mean that those who remain are subjected to work which is increasingly de-skilled, fragmented, alienating and stressful.

Because of the high rate of obsolescence indicated above, there is growing pressure for staff dealing with computers to accept shift-work[18].

Some of the medical and sociological effects of shiftworking which were described in the 1960s[19] are now beginning to be evident in the fields of white collar work. It has been suggested that those required to work rotating shifts experience an ulcer rate eight times higher than average, a divorce rate some 50% higher, and a juvenile delinquency rate in their children 80% higher than average[20]. Although a recent Government Report[21] dismisses some of these concerns, the evidence is that Trade Unions are now taking increasing action against the introduction of shiftwork (because structural unemployment grows simultaneously!).

The subjective concerns of those using computers are tending to grow. Journalists, for example, reported a feeling of isolation[22], whilst managers using an electronic office regarded the software as 'hostile'[23]. In Norway, workers at NEBB refused to use a range of terminals because they operated in a mode which was 'undirectional' and hence not responsive to the human being and, as they pointed out, was inherently undemocratic.*

Symbiosis?

Many perceptive computer users are now aware that they are being paced and controlled by the machine rather than the other way round. This in part results from a contradiction in the human/machine ineraction. The human being is the dialectical opposite of the machine in that he or she is slow, inconsistent, unreliable but highly creative. The machine on the other hand may be regarded as fast, consistent, reliable but totally non-creative[24]. Initially, these opposite characteristics were perceived as complementary and re-

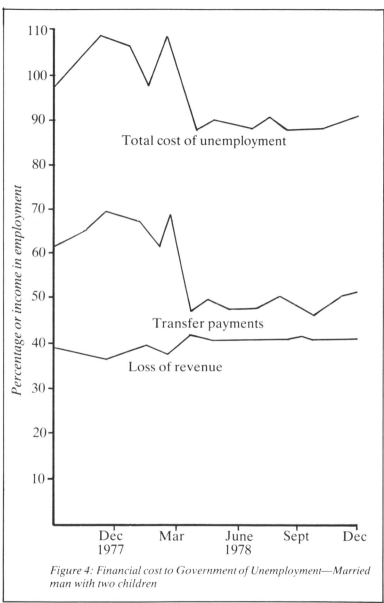

Figure 4: Financial cost to Government of Unemployment—Married man with two children

* For a thought-provoking analysis of some of the problems of computerisation in West Germany, see 15 in which he shows that in 1975 there was 90 000 000 000 DM of unused industrial potential, whilst at the same time computers were being frantically introduced to improve efficiency!

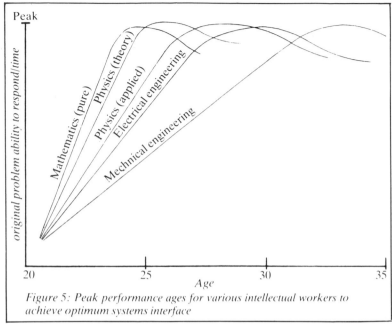

Figure 5: Peak performance ages for various intellectual workers to achieve optimum systems interface

garded as providing the basis for a perfect human/machine symbiosis[25].

Practice in recent years seems to suggest that the above is only partially correct. The computer dramatically increases the rate at which the quantitative is handled, and the stress upon the human being as he or she tries to make the qualitative judgements can be significant. In some instances the decision-making rate is forced up 19 times. Experiments have shown that those working interactively with computers in the field of engineering design find this interaction so intense that their creativity decreases by 30% to 40% in the first hour and 80% in the second hour[26].

This general tendency has resulted in the International Labour Office recommending safeguards against nervous fatigue for white collar workers[27]. An IFIP Working Party has actually suggested that mental hazards 'caused by inhumanly designed computer systems should be regarded as a punishable offence just as endangering the bodily safety'. Yet the tendency is to work out the peak performance ages of human beings so that they can be most effectively interfaced with the equipment, and this is true of even highly scientific and technical staff. Those who slow down are regarded as a bottleneck to the system (see Figures 5 and 6). There are then grounds for believing that the overwork of some becomes the objective basis for the lack of any work for others.

Computers and Taylorism

The computer is a convenient 'Trojan horse' with which to introduce into intellectualwork the division and Taylorism which leads to the dehumanisation which has already been evident in the field of manual work when it was subdivided into narrow alienated tasks. Yet Taylorism is the very essence of Scienntific Management, and as its originator, Frederick Taylor, pointed out:

> 'In my system, the workman is told minutely what he is to do and how he is to do it, and any improvement he makes upon the instructions given to him is fatal to success.'

Many computer scientists are surprised to learn that it was the founder of their industry, Charles Babbage, who anticipated Taylor in the field of intellectual work and said:

> 'We may have already mentioned what may perhaps appear paradoxical to some of our readers, that the division of labour can be applied with equal success to mental as well as mechanical operations, and that it ensures in both the same economy of time'[29].

Taylorism is now spreading rapidly through the fields of intellectual work, either overtly or covertly. Techniques have been developed to measure the rate at which people think and distinguish between the passive reception of visual input (seeing) and the active recep-

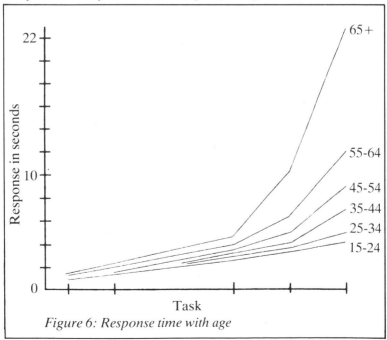

Figure 6: Response time with age

tion (looking), as well as the passive reception of audio signals (hearing) and the active reception (listening)[30]. These same techniques are spreading through the entire spectrum of intellectual work from routine clerical tasks to quite complicated intellectual activities, such as design, and are tending to reduce intellectual work to 'the mental production line'. Indeed Howard Carlson, a psychiatrist employed by General Motors said, 'the computer may be to middle management what the assembly line is to the hourly paid works[31].'

The computer has provided a framework in which these techniques can invade even the most non-alienated areas of intellectual work such as that of university professors.

The well-known Frank Wolfe algorithm is now used to work out the efficiency and performance of university professors. This is done within an organisational framework in which the university is regarded in the form of a factory model. The recruitment of students is referred to as 'materal procurement', examinations as 'quality control' and graduation as 'delivery'. The professors are of course referred to as 'operators[32]'.

It may be felt that this notion of the worker being reduced to an appendage of the machine or the process is an exaggeration of what is happening. Let us look at what Robert Boguslaw has had to say about this process:

'Our immediate concern, let us remember, is the exploitation of the operator unit approach to systems design no matter what materials are used. We must take care to prevent this discussion from degenerating into the single sided analysis of the complex characteristics of one type of systems material, namely human beings. What we need is an inventory of the way in which behaviour can be controlled, and a description of some of the instruments which will help us to achieve that control. If this provides us with sufficient handles on human materials so that we can think of them as we think of metal parts, electrical power or chemical reactions, then we have succeeded in placing human material on the same footing as any other material and can begin to proceed with our problems of systems design... There are, however, many disadvatages in the use of human operating units. They are somewhat fragile, they are subject to fatigue, obsolescence, disease and even death. They are frequently stupid, unreliable and limited in memory capacity; but beyond all this, they sometimes seek to design their own circuitry. This in a material is unforgivable, and any system utilising them must devise appropriate safeguards[33].'

Thus, that which is most precious about human beings – the ability

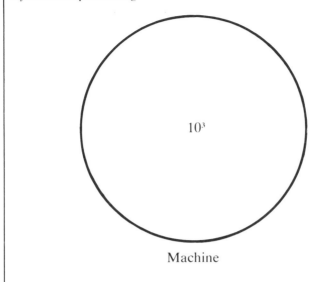

Figure 7: Comparison of units of 'intelligence' available for total information processing

10^3

Machine

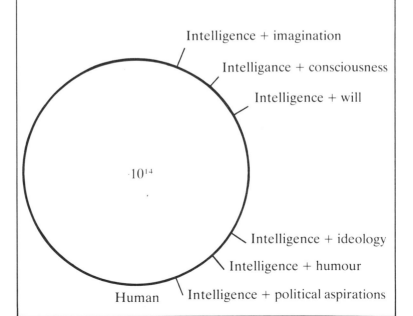

Intelligence + imagination

Intelligance + consciousness

Intelligence + will

10^{14}

Intelligence + ideology

Intelligence + humour

Human

Intelligence + political aspirations

to 'design their own circuitry' or think for themselves – is now said to be an attribute which should be suppressed by the technology. These organisational developments raise profound political and social questions about the nature and form of work itself, but also fundamental issues such as individual freedom and the right of the individual to develop his or her capabilities to the full.

De-Skilling

The scale and nature of the de-skilling which accompanies these forms of technological change have been described in a historical setting[34]. The de-skilling stretches right through the intellectual field. One researcher who examined the effects of computerisation in Swedish banks stated that 'increased automation converted tellers, who were in fact minibankers, into automatons'[35]. In a detailed report on the wider societal effects of computerisation, the author has shown that even architects using computer-aided architectual design systems are de-skilled[36].

It is sometimes argued in defence of these developments that at least in the 'occupational growth areas' associated with computing and particularly in jobs associated with the issuing of instructions to computers, employees will be undertaking work of growing skill and creativity. To suggest this would be to fail completely to understand the historical tendency to de-skill *all* work. Programming itself is being reduced to routines, and 'the de-skiller is de-skilled' as structured programming breaks with the universal (if short) tradition of idiosyncratic software production[37].

Further to this, there are strong indications that those elements which are normally regarded as constituting industrial alienation – particularly powerlessness, meaninglessness, loss of self and normlessness[38,39] – are now increasingly present in computerised environments. There are also grounds for believing that the creativity of the workers involved is diminished by the tightly constrained and systematised work environments associated with these highly computerised systems. These tend to induce methods of work and problem-solving techniques that are remarkably at variance with the circumstances and attributes which appear to have contributes to creativity both in the arts and in the sciences when viewed historically[40,41,42].

The problems of employment, or indeed unemployment, which arise from computerisation, provide a unique aperture through which we can view the problems of this type of technology as a whole.

There is already sufficient evidence about to indicate clearly that computer science, like science in general, is not value-free or neutral, and that as we design systems, we making a whole series of assumptions about human beings and society. Either consciously or unconsciously, our design methodology is such that we seek to eliminate people and human intelligence from these processes. Yet, viewed in terms of total information retrieval, assembly, pattern recognition and processing, the systems currently available or even conceived at a throretical level are trivial compared with human intelligence in the wider sense of that word (see Figure 8). Some members of the computer fraternity are now questioning fundamentally where all this is leading us [43, 44].

The exponential rate of technological change makes this debate all the more urgent, otherwise we may find that options now open to us may become permanently closed off. These were the fears of the founding father of cybernetics, Norbert Wiener, when he cautioned 'although machines are theoretically subject to human criticism, such criticism may be ineffective until long after it is relevant'[45].

The important issue to realise that there are options open to us, and that we should not allow ourselves to be swept along by the internal dynamism of the technology. The future is not 'out there' in the sense in which America was out there before Columbus went to discover it. The future is not pre-determined, nor does it have prescribed boundaries and forms. It is yet to be made by human beings, and as we start to construct it we must never allow outselves to be so facinated by the technology and the systems that we forget what it is really about, which is people.

Human Centred Systems

It is vital that we demonstrate that there are alternatives to the growing structural unemployment and the de-skilling associated with new technology in its given form. The Lucas Aerospace workers have convincingly demonstrated some of the options open to society by proposing (and in some cases actually building prototypes) a range of socially useful products which should be manufactured as an alternative to the degradation of unemployment. They emphasised that they should be produced in forms of work organisation which link hand and brain, are human enhancing and liberatory[46, 47].

It is significant that the French Government proposes to build upon elements of the Lucas workers' proposals[48] whilst the Greater London Council is attempting a highly imaginative and radical restructuring of Science, Technology and Manufacturing which draws heavily on the Lucas philosophy[49] as a major component of its London Industrial Strategy.

Campaigns of this kind provide trade unionists with a framework which far transcends the narrow economism which has characterised them for too long. They can and should extend industrial relations to include the fundamental design assumptions built into the systems. Space permits only one example each of manual and intellectual work to illustrate the point.

Manual Work

Over the past 200 years, turning has been one of the highly skilled jobs to be found in most engineering workshops. Toolroom turning is one of the most highly skilled jobs of all. The historical tendency, certainly since the was, has been, to de-skill this function by using numerical controlled machines. This is done by part programming – a process by which the desired N.C. tool motions are converted to finished tapes. Conventional (symbolic) part programming languages require that a part programmer, upon deciding how a part is to be machined, describes the desired tool motions by a series of symbolic commands. These commands are used to define geometric entities, that is points, lines and surfaces, which may be given symbolic names. In practice, the part programming languages require the operator to synthesise the desired tool motion from a restricted available vocabulary of symbolic commands. However, all this is doing is attempting to build into the machine the intelligence that would have been exercised by a skilled worker in going through the labour process.

It is possible, by using computerised equipment in a symbiotic way, to link it to the skills of a human being and define the tool motions without symbolic description. Such a method is called Analogic Part Programming[50]. In this type of part programming, tool motion information is conveyed in analogic form by turning a crank or moving a joystick or some other hand/eye coordination task using readout with precision adequate for the machining process.

Using a dynamic visual display of the entire working area of the machine tool including the workpiece, the fixturing, the cutting tool and its position, the skilled craftsman can directly input the desired tool motions to 'machine' the workpiece in the display. Such a system, which may be described as "Part Programming by doing" would represent a sharp contrast to the main historical tendency towards Symbolic Part Programming. It would require no knowledge of conventional part programming languages, because the necessity to describe symbolically the desired tool motions would be eliminated. This is achieved by providing a system whereby the information regarding a cut is conveyed in a manner closely resembling the conceptual process of the skilled machinist. Thus it would be necessary to maintain and enhance the skill and ability of a range of people who would work in parallel with the system.

Significant research has been carried out in these fields[51], yet in spite of its obvious advantages it has not been received with any enthusiasm by large corporations or indeed funding bodies. That this is so would appear to be an entirely political judgement rather than a technological one.

Intellectual Work

In the field of intellectual work, Rosenbrock has questioned the underlying assumptions of the manner in which we are developing aided design systems. He charges firstly, that the present techniques fail to exploit the opportunity which interactive computing can offer. The computer and the human mind have quite different but complementary abilities. The computer excels in analysis and numerical computation. The human mind excels in pattern recognition, the assessment of complicated situations and the intuitive leap to new solutions. If these different abilities can be combined, they amount to something much more powerful and effective than anything we have had before.

Rosenbrock objects to the 'Automated Manual' type of system since it represents as he says "a loss of nerve, a loss of belief in human abilities, and a further unthinking application of the doctrine of the Division of Labour"[52].

As in the case of turning described above, Rosenbrock sees two paths open in respect of design. The first is to accept the skill and

knowledge of the designed, and attempt to give designers improved techniques and improved facilities for exercising their knowledge and skill. Such a system would demand a truly interactive use of computers in a way that allows the very different capabilities of the computer and the human mind to be used to the full.

The alternative to this, he suggests, is to "subdivide and codify the design process, incoporating the knowledge of the existing designers so that it is reduced to a sequence of simple choices"[53]. This he points out, would lead to a de-skilling such that the job can be done by a person with less training and less experience. Rosenbrock has demonstrated the first human enhancing alternative by developing a C.A.D. system with graphic output to develop displays from which the designer can assess stability, speed of response, sensitivity to disturbance and other properties of the system.

If, having looked at the displays, the performance of the system is not satisfactory, the displays will suggest how it may be improved. In this respect the displays carry on the long tradition of early pencil and paper methods but of course they bring with them much greater computing power. Thus, as with the lathe and the skilled turner, so also with the V.D.U. and the designer, possibilities exist of a symbiotic relationship between the worker and the equipment. In both cases, tacit knowledge and experience is accepted as valid and is enhanced and developed.

In Rosenbrock's case it was necessary to examine the underlying mathematical techniques involved in control systems design[54]. The outcome of his work does demonstrate in embryo that there are other alternatives if we are prepared to explore them, and he has suggested that we are now at a unique historical turning point when we may close off options which are now open to us. This process he describes as the "Lushai Hills Effect".

These examples have been quoted in order to demonstrate that it is possible to so design systems as to enhance human beings rather than to diminish them and subordinate them to the machine. It is my view that systems of this kind, however desirable they may be, will not be developed and widely applied since they challenge power structures in society. Those who have power in society, epitomised by the vast multinational coporations, are concerned with extending their power and gaining control over human beings rather than with liberating thcm Such a viewpoint may appear abnormally sectarian or political to some readers, yet they only have to look at the headlines of the technical press to see statements which completely reinforce that analysis. Thus a headline in the ENGINEER stated "People are trouble, but machines obey"[55] and even in economic papers one finds headlines such as "Robots don't strike"[56].

The reality is that as we design technological systems, we are designing sets of social relationships, and as we question those social relationships and attempt to design systems differently, we are then beginning to challenge in a political way power structures in society. The alternatives are stark. Either we will have a future in which human beings are reduced to a sort of bee-like behaviour, reacting to the systems and equipment specified for them; or we will have a future in which masses of people, conscious of their skills and abilities in both a political and technical sense, decide that they are going to be the architects of a new form of technological development which will enhance human creativity and mean more freedom of choice rather than less [57]. The truth is, we shall have to make the profound political decision as to whether we intend to act as architects or behave like bees.

REFERENCES

1. Cooley, M.J.E. *The knowledge worker in the 1980s*, Diebold Research Programme, Conf Proc Doc no EC35,Amsterdam (Nov 1975)
2. Fabrican, S. *Measurement of technoligical change*, US Dept of Labor, Washington (1965)
3. Elliott, J. and Lloyd, J. *The microelectronics debate*, Financial Times, (Dec 7 1978)
4. Owen, K. *Professor shows how technology will change society*, The Times p.23 (Nov 13 1978)
5. Computer Weekly, p.3 (Sept 21 1978)
6. Barker, J. and Downing, H. *Office automation – word processing and the transformation of patriarchal relations*, CAITS North East London Polytechnic (Jan 1979)
7. *Employment and word processing*, Report of Working Group 1, APEX London (1978)
8. Lavick, J.J. *CAD: a Trade Union viewpoint*, (M.J.E. Cooley) Proc CAD '76 IPC Science and Technology Press Guildford (1976)
9. Bennett, P. Computer Weekly, p.13 (Feb 8 1979)
10. Holland, G. Computer Weekly, p.3 (Jan 25 1979)
11. Carter Sir Charles, The Times, p.23 (Nov 23 1978)
12. Ashworth, J. Computing, p.18 (Feb 1 1979)
13. Yankelovich, D. *The changing values on campus*, Square Press New York, p.171 (1972)
14. George, M. *The future of employment in engineering and manufacture*, Centre for Alternative Industrial and Technological Systems, NE London Polytechnic (Nov 1978)
15. Briefs, U. *Systems and workers*, in *Data Exchange*, (Diebold Research Program-Europe) p.4-16, (Sept/Oct 1976)
16. Fletcher, R. *Social democracy and unemployment*, Proc, *Alternatives to unemployment*, Conf NE London Polytechnic (Nov 18 1978)
17. Buschluter, S. *German steel workers to strike*, Guardian p.21 (Nov 27 1978)

18. Health and Safety Executive, *Shiftwork and health; a critical review of the literature*, Report London (1978)
19. Mott, P.E. *Shift work, the social psychology and physical consequence*, Ann Arbor (1974)
20. Cooley, M.J.E. *Taylor in the office*, in *Humanising the workplace*, R.N. Ottoway (ed), Croom Helm Ltd, London (1977)
21. Health and Safety Executive, *Shiftwork and health; a critical review of the literature*, Report, London (1978)
22. Computing, *Making sure technology is right for the press*, Computing p.14, March 23, 1978)
23. Computer Weekly, *Electronic office system designed to improve manager's productivity*, Computer Weekly, p.12 (Dec 21, 1978)
24. Cooley, M.J.E. PhD Thesis, NE London Polytechnic (unpublished)
25. Licklider, J.C.R. *Man-computer symbiosis*, IRE Trans Electrom 2, pp.4-11 (1960)
26. Bernholz, A. Proc CAD Conf LFIP, Eindhoven, Netherlands (1973)
27. IFIP *Human choice and computers*, Report GCC Lp5 Proc IFIP, Vienna (1974)
28. Taylor, F.W. *The art of cutting metals*, ASME, New York (1906)
29. Babbagem, C. *On the economy of machinery and manufactures*, New York (reprint) (1963)
30. *A classification and terminology of mental work*, Workstudy (June 1974)
31. Carlson, H.C. *Labour and monopoly capital*, (H. Braverman), Monthly Review Press, New York (1974)
32. Cooley, M.J.E. *The university as a factory*, New Scientist vol 70 no. 1006 pp.708-709 (June 24, 1976)
33. Bogulsaw, R. *Contradictions of science and technology*, (M.J.E. Cooley) in *Ideology of/in the natural sciences*, Rose and Rose (eds) Macmillan Press, London vol 1, (Political Economy of Science) pp.72-95 (1976)
34. Braverman, H. *Labour and monopoly capital*, Monthly Review Press, New York (1974)
35. Docherty, P. *Automation in the service industries*, Round Table Discussion IFAC, Reported in IFAC Social Effects Newsletter no. 6 p.7 (Sept 1978)
36. Cooley, M.J.E. *Some social effects of computerisation*, in *Man/Communication*, State of the Art Report Infotech, Maidenhead UK (1979)
37. Kraft, P. *Programmes and managers — the routinisation of computer programming in the United States*, Springer Verlag, Berlin, Heidelberg, New York (1977)
38. Seeman, M. *On the meaning of alienation*, American Sociological Review, vol 24 no. 6, pp.783-791 (Dec 1959)
39. Shacht, R. *Alienation*, Anchor Books, New York (1970)
40. Beveridge, W.I.B. *The art of scientific investigation*, Mercury Books, London (1961)
41. Eiseley, L. *The mind as nature*, Harper and Row, New York (1962)
42. Fabun, D. *You and creativity*, Kaiser Aluminum News, vol 25 no.3
43. Rosenbrock, H.H. *The future of control*, Automatica vol 13 (1977)
44. Weizenbaum, J. *Computer power and human reason*, W.H. Freeman and Co, San Francisco (1976)
45. Wiener, N. Science 131 p.1355 (1960)
46. Cooley, M.J.E. *Architect or Bee?* Langley Technical Services, Slough Berks, 1980)
47. Wainwright, H. & Elliott, D. *The Lucas Plan: A New Trade Unionism in the Making*, Allison & Busby, London 1982
48. Palmer, J. *French boost for alternative work pioneers*, The Guardian 24.7.81
49. Palmer, J. *Technology Networks*, Report by the Chief Economic Adviser I&E Committee, July Mtg 1982
50. Gossard & Von Turkovich, *Analogic Part Programming with Interactive Graphics*, Annals of the C.I.R.P. Vol 27, Jan 1978

51. Gossard, D. *Analogic Part Programming with Interactive Graphics*, PhD Thesis M.I.T. February 1975
52. Rosenbrock, H.H. *The Future of Control* Proc 6th IFAC Congress, Boston (1976), Reprint in Automatica vol 13 (1977)
53. Rosenbrock, H.H. *Interactive Computing – A New Opportunity*, Control Systems Centre Report No 388, U.M.I.S.T. 1977
54. Rosenbrock, H.H. *Computer Aided Control Systems Design*, Academic Press, London, N.Y. San Francisco 1974
55. Reported in *The Engineer*, 14th September 1978, p.24, 25
56. Reported in *The Economist*, 14th July, 1973 p.71
57. Cooley, M.J.E. op cit (47)

MANAGING THE PROCESS OF CHANGE
DAVID FAIRBAIRN

There are close to 3.2 million people unemployed in this country. The question is: what can information technology do about it? But before attempting to answer that, I should make clear two points about my own stance.

There are three current predictions, emanating from the Universities of London, Cambridge and Liverpool, about where unemployment will lie over the next three to five years. The least optimistic of these suggests that it will rise to something over 3.5 million. I am even more pessimistic than the most pessimistic of these predictions; I do not think there is any natural order of events that can reverse the present trend of unemployment unless we do something about it. Therefore, I do not start from a position of natural optimism.

Secondly, I do not think this is primarily an economic question. Work means doing something for the benefit of others. Getting paid is not necessarily the essence of it. The essence is that we are doing it for others as distinct from doing, say, the same thing for leisure where we do it for our own benefit. So work is of crucial importance to individuals and it is no substitute to pay them to do nothing. That is to deny people the ability to perform services for others, and it is very demotivating. I do not therefore see leisure – particularly enforced leisure – as an acceptable substitute for work. The question that we have to address is whether we are moving into a world where that has to be accepted. Conventional wisdom today suggests that there is perhaps a finite amount of work to do, and that we are somehow running out of it. The impact of technology, so the argument goes, is to limit the amount of work that has to be done; we simply have to say to people, "Sorry, there is no work for you".

That concept is the most profound nonsense. If we look around us, we live in sub-standard houses, we drive on sub-standard roads, we use sub-standard railways. We send our children to school in sub-standard educational systems, and when we are sick we go into hospitals which are woefully sub-standard. So on what conceivable basis do we tell people there is no useful work for them to perform? To state that there is overproduction, that there is nothing to do, is exactly the converse of the truth. We have the absurdity of a mountain of unperformed work on the one hand, and on the other a mountain of unused people. Why?

There is, of course, a fairly obvious solution, and that is to put pound notes into the hands of the people whose needs are unsatisfied. That will create the demand which will create employment for others. Keynes thought of it, and, in a sense, in the 1930s and 1940s, he got it right. But there is a snag. When we put pound notes into the hands of people under those circumstances, instead of creating a rapid increase in output we create a rapid rise in prices – massive inflation.

There is something strange about the way Britain's economic system currently works. To draw an analogy, if you have a car which is advanced in years or perhaps not too well tuned and you put your foot down hard on the accelerator when you want to move away, it splutters and stalls. Put your foot on the pedal gradually and it can take up the increase in fuel flow, but you have to keep the rate of acceleration down to what the system can take. This is fundamentally the problem we have with the economy; a problem of the rate of change we can accommodate. The tragic position at the moment is that the economy appears to be able to accommodate only a low rate of change without going into a stall – about 1½% or 2%. But the rate that is necessary to keep anything close to full employment is 3% or more.

Looking back to the 1930s, particularly in the United States, exactly the same predictions were being made then as are made today. People said that because of the automation of production on the shop floor, the requirement for work had been permanently diminished and that there would always be high levels of unemployment. But by the 1950s, it became clear that that was total nonsense. The process of adaptation and change had taken place by then.

Economic growth means, as Adam Smith put it in the 18th century, making two blades of grass grow where one grew before. That is steadily happening, and there is a very good historical basis for saying that demand does keep pace with supply. However, it does not do so automatically and immediately, and the processes by which it does tend to be slow, particularly where adaptation has to take place. Take the example of the motor car. Seventy years ago it took two years to make a car; today you can make one in two weeks. That does not mean that we now employ one-fiftieth of the number of people who used to make motor cars — we employ 200 times as many, making 10,000 times as many cars. This is the characteristic of much of what we have done in terms of physical production.

But the issue of physical production is now almost an irrelevance — it belongs to the early part of this century. In 1967 a very important thing happened in the United States: for the first time, 50% of the gross national product no longer came from producing goods: the balance had tipped towards a service economy. It has since gone decisively further in that direction, and we are now in the

position where most of the things we want to spend our money on — schools, hospitals, education, services of all kinds — do not lend themselves to processes of mechanisation and mass production.

We suffer a major problem, but the key difficulty lies in our inability to speed up change. What the world is doing at the moment is slowing down the speed of progress in order to keep inflation within acceptable limits. That is not a satisfactory solution, though. Its consequences can only be described as disastrous and demotivating.

What the problem amounts to is an inability to manage the process of change; and the process of change is essentially concerned with the process of decision-taking. Whether it is new products or whether it is adaptation from one form of technology to another, we are suffering from a massive shortage of the ability to handle information effectively. It is particularly interesting to look at the example of Japan, which has been much more successful, both in handling the process of change and — very significantly — in maintaining a very high level of employment. In Japan, they employ five times as many people in the business of analysing the decisions that have been taken. In marketing and production planning they are much more labour-intensive; but then they take less than half the time to get a product into production and institute the process of change. So they get twice the speed of change, and at the same time redeploy people into those other activities.

The Fujitsu company now have robots making robots. But when asked, "Are you displacing people?", their answer was "No". As far as they are concerned, the robots are the shopfloor workers. But Fujitsu are massively increasing the number of people employed in working out how they should develop and run their business.

We must take a radically different view about the way in which we handle information — both the speed and the accuracy of it — in taking decisions. The solution lies not on the shopfloor, but in the process of decision-taking, in the brainwork. We have to deploy technology massively to solve this set of problems, but the technology has the ability to do it. And we will see as a consequence not a reduction in the numbers of people employed in these activities, but a very substantial increase. We have seen that increase in banking, we have seen it in the public service, and if we tackle the problem of information handling in the decision-taking part of the economy it will serve two purposes. We will secure a growth of employment in that extremely important sector, and we will succeed in speeding up the rate of change. That will adapt us to the point at which we shall be back, by about 1987 or 1988 if we take the right decisions now, to full employment at the levels we enjoyed in the 1940s and 1950s. That is what information technology can do, and there is no more important task for it to tackle.

Privacy: A free or secret state?

IT's ability to store and collate data on a massive scale brings greatly increased risks of state abuse. Who will control and who will have access to flow of confidential personal information? Britain lags behind other countries in establishing data protection laws, but is there any evidence to show that privacy laws are enforcable anyway? The Lindop Committee recommended the formation of an Independent Data Protection Authority. The Home Office and the Metropolitan Police are in favour of exemption from privady legislation for security systems and police files. The present government has rejected the Lindop proposals in favour of its own 'ombudsman' approach detailed in a White Paper this Spring. But the paper is seen in some quarters as vague, and its proposals for a single independent registrar, appointed by the Crown, as ineffectual.

Chairman: Charles N. Read. Speakers: Paul Sieghart, Patricia Hewitt, John Dawson, Ralph Shuffrey.

THE DATA PROTECTION DEBATE

The debate about computers and privacy was the first to become polarised between those who saw computers as God's greatest gift to mankind since Eve, and those who saw them only as tools for evil men who would use them to make the world an even worse place than it was before. Indeed, the very juxtaposition of the two words 'computers' and 'privacy' has come to imply an antithesis, a conflict, a tug-of-war − as if the 'and' were a form of 'versus' in some ritual battle which one or the other side had to win.

But the technology has moved a long way on since that debate began, and all over the world enormous quantities of data about identifiable individuals are now stored and processed in computers. The genie is out of the bottle, and there is no way of putting it back again. What we must now find urgently is a way of harnessing all this effort for our own benefit, and of protecting ourselves from its dangers − in the words of Bing Crosby's song of long ago, 'to accentuate the positive and eliminate the negative' (though in most cases it is probably starry-eyed to imagine that we can ever do more than *mitigate* the negative, rather than eliminate it altogether).

For computers as for any other technology, the golden keys lie in the right form of social regulation – not of the inanimate computers themselves, but of the uses to which animate beings might be tempted to put them. As Lord Scarman pointed out some years ago, the computer has much in common in this respect with the motor car – another machine from which we derive great benefits, but which also presents dangers for all of us. What we must learn to do in all those cases is to control the activities of those who control the machines.

That of course is precisely what 'data protection' legislation sets out to achieve. The title is welcome, since it points the way forward from the polarised antithesis of 'computers *versus* privacy' to a synthesis in which everyone's legitimate interests can be suitably protected – the interests of the user of a computerised information system which processes personal data (the 'data user') no less than the interests of the people whose data are being processed (the 'data subjects'). As the Lindop Committee put it in a sentence as important as it was inelegant, the whole object of the exercise is 'that the right people (and only the right people) are able to use the right personal information (and only the right personal information) for the right purposes (and only the right purposes)'!

Some gum-trees

How the debate has moved from the antithesis to the synthesis may one day provide some insights for a future historian of ideas. If you start with a single concern for people's privacy, you will call for the most powerful regulation of all computers which handle personal data. But then, if you are a computer user, you will instantly ask 'Why pick on me?' – especially if your application is not only harmless, but positively beneficial (and there are many of those) – and point out that we already live in a grossly over-regulated society, and that every new regulation is another brake on enterprise, costs more money, and multiplies bureaucracies. If you regulate everything in sight, you will only succeed in throwing out the baby with the bath water.

Or, if you happen to be a member of the computing profession – a data processing manager, say – you will understandably complain that it is anyway not your computer which presents the risk, but the things which your boss is telling you to use it for, and that it would be grossly unfair to make you personally responsible simply for carrying out his perfectly lawful orders.

Faced with such objections, the enthusiast for regulation tries another tack: why not distinguish between 'public' and 'private' information, and only regulate the second? Unfortunately, that too turns out to be more difficult than it looks. One's name, one might think for example, can hardly be 'private'. But suppose some malign or over-zealous person adds it to a list of other names under the heading 'Persons suspected of subversive homosexual fascist activities', which he consults every time he is asked to approve a candidate for employment, or insurance, or a housing allocation? And what goes for names goes equally for addresses: I might, for example, not wish it to be widely known that my current address is the local mental hospital, let alone the local prison.

It soon turns out that there is no mileage in trying to distinguish 'private' from 'public' information – or even to try to rank different kinds of personal information in some order of 'sensitivity'. (In any case, different people in different societies at different times will often not rank such information about themselves in the same way.) So here is another gum-tree which we must leave behind as we travel along the road, having climbed it and come down again, sadder but perhaps a little wiser. Before we do, though, we can find confirmation for an earlier insight: 'information' is always an association between data – technically called a 'concatenation' – rather than the data themselves. By itself, the datum which constitutes my name is neutral and tells others nothing. They only get information about me if that name is associated with some other datum or data, such as the address of Her Majesty's Prison, or the name of someone else's wife combined with a particular hotel room on a particular night, or the purchase of a hammer the day before her husband was mysteriously found in the woods with a large hole in his head.

Regulating tasks

The risks to privacy therefore do not lie in data by themselves, but in the way in which they are concatenated – or, more generally, 'processed' or 'handled' – for some specific purpose. So if there is to be regulation in order to eliminate (or even mitigate) the negative in the processing of personal data, what has to be regulated is not the computers, or the data stored in them, or their users, but the tasks – technically called the 'applications' – which the users instruct the computers to perform on the data. That is the first golden key to any sensible data protection scheme.

Next, there is the problem of whether you regulate every computerised task performed on personal data by the same rules applied with equal strictness, or whether there are some criteria by which you can vary either the rules, or their strictness, in accordance with the tasks to which they are to apply. And here, if you take the trouble to survey the personal data processing scene, you make two quite reassuring discoveries. The first is that there is only a comparatively small number of *categories* of tasks – payrolls, say, or current account banking, or membership records. (The Lindop Committee, having surveyed the field pretty thoroughly, guessed that there were probably no more than about 50 such general categories.) But the second discovery is more reassuring still: it is that the overwhelming bulk of applications are what I like to call 'subject-friendly' – that is, that the interests of the data user coincide largely, and often entirely, with those of the data subject. My bank, for example, has exactly the same interests as I have: that postings to my account should be prompt and accurate, and that both the bank manager and I should be able to find out the current state of the account whenever we want to. Interestingly, the bank also shares my concern that others should not be able to get at this information if they have no business to: if a bank's information system about its customers were shown to be 'leaky' in this way, it would rapidly lose its customers to the competition across the High Street.

The same holds true even for the government computers which so many dread, operated by their equally dreaded faceless officials. The great majority of these are in fact just as subject-friendly as most of those in the private sector: the principal concern of the DHSS system at Newcastle, for instance, is that its beneficiaries should promptly get all the benefits to which they are entitled. Similarly, clinical information in NHS computers is held and processed there simply in order that the patients can be more effectively and efficiently treated for their complaints. And most of the many computer tasks in local government are designed to give people better services at lower cost.

Openness

So, to quite a large extent, one ought to be able to rely on the co-operation of the data users, because they mostly share their data subjects' interests. But there are some exceptions, and that of course is where the trouble starts. For instance, there is the user who is either incompetent or misperceives his own interest. He may have a leaky information system simply because he has never spent enough thought – or money – on making it as secure as it needs to be, given the data that he holds there, their value to him, and the tasks that someone else could run on them. Or he may pursue a short-term interest to the detriment of a long-term one, such as selling information to outsiders in order to make a quick buck, hoping his customers will not find out.

Even for inherently subject-friendly systems, therefore, there

has to be *some* regulation to protect the data subjects from the odd fool or the even rarer knave. But that is easy and cheap to do: all that is needed is to define what one might call the 'best practice' among the users, make sure that they all know what it is, and see to it that they will apply it as much for their own protection as for their data subjects'. That requires, above all, full consultation with all the interests concerned, and full openness, in the drafting and implementation of data protection rules – and that is the second golden key. One great benefit from using it is that it greatly reduces the costs to the users of complying with the rules, and often helps to improve their systems to their own advantage, as well as their data subjects'.

Finally, one comes to the few inherently 'subject-hostile' applications. In the private sector, one thinks of the credit-reporting and other 'black-listing' applications, whose users' interests are diametrically opposed to those of 'their' data subjects. In the public sector one thinks of whatever systems are operated by the security services, of police intelligence systems, immigration control and suchlike. Here, there is a major conflict between the data user and the data subject, just as there might have been the odd minor conflict in the case of subject-friendly applications run by the odd fool or the rare knave. How then is such a conflict to be resolved?

Independence

And here we come to the third, and crucial, golden key to any sensible data protection system. It is a commonplace, both of law and of real life, that no one must be a judge in his own cause – for the simple reason that, if he is, his decisions are likely to be wrong, and certain not to be credible. So, for all cases of that kind, what is needed is some independent and impartial judge or arbitrator to adjudicate between the conflicting interests. In short, both he who makes the rules and he who applies them must be, and be seen to be, independent both of data users and of data subjects.

And, since government (both central and local) is one of the largest users of computerised personal information systems — including some of the most subject-hostile systems — that means that whoever makes or applies data protection rules must both be, and be seen to be, independent of government. At the same time, these are public functions, and whoever performs them must be made accountable in some public forum. In our constitutional system, that can only be Parliament, and whoever is put in charge of data protection should therefore be an officer answerable direct to Parliament, much like the Parliamentary Commissioner for Administration (the Ombudsman) or the Comptroller and Auditor-General.

The White Paper

It is one of the minor ironies of the way in which our machinery of government is currently structured that most of the subject-hostile systems in the public sector happen to come under the responsibility of the Home Office, the very Department of State which is also charged with the protection of the liberties of the subject, and therefore of data protection — which may perhaps help to explain why we shall be the last of the major industrialised countries of Western Europe to install data protection legislation.

But it must be said in all fairness that the Home Office too has travelled far along the learning curve since it first started to look seriously at this subject. Put under pressure from all our European trading partners in the Council of Europe who have now agreed on an International Data Protection Convention, and from a remarkable national alliance of industry, commerce, the trade unions, the consumers, the professions and the privacy lobby — not to mention just about every other Government Department in Whitehall — even the Home Office now accepts the urgent need for a comprehensive data protection law. The White Paper it published in April of this year shows that the three golden keys have all been officially recognised, and that at least the appropriate blanks for them have been fashioned in order that they can eventually open the locks. What is now needed is some detailed filing in order to ensure that the keys will really fit the locks, and will go on doing so for the foreseeable future.

That White Paper, of course, is only the culmination of a long history. As far back as the 1960s, Private Members' Bills were being introduced in Parliament. The Younger Committee was appointed in 1970, and reported in 1972. In 1975, the then government published an earlier White Paper, promising legislation based on all three of the golden keys. In 1976, it appointed the Lindop Committee, which reported in 1978 with detailed proposals for this legislation. Meanwhile, European and other countries were already enacting their own data protection laws, and in order to harmonise those laws and ensure the free flow of information between them they adopted the Council of Europe Convention, with which our own legislation must now comply.

That Convention sets out certain general principles of data protection, designed to protect the interests of all the parties concerned. Those in turn were largely based on the Lindop principles. They now read as follows:—

   (i) The information shall be obtained and processed fairly and lawfully;

  (ii) It shall be held for a specified and legitimate purpose or purposes;

 (iii) It shall not be used or disclosed in a way incompatible with those purposes;

 (iv) It shall be adequate, relevant, and not excessive in relation to the specified purposes;

  (v) It shall be accurate and, where necessary, kept up to date;

 (vi) It shall be kept in name-linked form for no longer than is necessary for the specified purposes;

(vii) The data subject shall have access to information held about him and be entitled to its correction or erasure where the legal provisions safeguarding personal data have not been complied with;

(viii) Appropriate security measures must be taken against unauthorised access, alteration or dissemination, accidental loss and accidental or unauthorised destruction of data.

What now remains to be done is to enact a system of regulation which will ensure that all users – in the public as well as the private sector – will observe these principles. It was to the details of that system that the discussion at this session was largely addressed. Perhaps to everyone's surprise, there were no great clashes of view. At least in this corner of the field, a synthesis now seems possible. Despite the fears that so many have expressed, it looks as if solutions to such problems *can* be found – provided enough people take enough trouble to do the hard and detailed work of thinking them out, promoting them, and ultimately installing and operating them.

   Here, just for once, there are grounds for optimism.

* Based on Paul Sieghart's contribution as a speaker at this session.

WHAT'S IN A FILE?
PATRICIA HEWITT

NCCL's interest is in protecting information privacy. We would define that as your right, as far as possible, to control personal information about yourself, to control who you give that information to, on what terms, and how it is subsequently used.

The problems that we would identify, in terms of breaching information privacy, are first of all secrecy: information may be held on you and used to make decisions about you without your even knowing that the records exist, or that you're the subject of an information-gathering exercise. Secondly, that the information may simply be wrong, irrelevant or out of date, and therefore may be used unfairly to make a decision about you. And thirdly, though this may appear paradoxical, that the information may not in fact be kept confidential. All too often we find that when civil servants in particular say that a personal record is 'confidential', they mean that it is confidential against *you* — you, the data-subject, can't see it — but almost anyone else who might be thought to have an interest in the matter can.

Those three central problems are very well illustrated by the case of Jan Martin, which some of you may have seen on *Panorama* last year. Jan was the perfect answer to the common question: "Surely, if you've nothing to hide, then you've nothing to fear from data banks?" Jan had nothing to hide. She applied for a job, and was offered one, at a private film company which made training films for private industrial clients. Subsequently her employer, a former BBC television producer, was telephoned by one of his industrial clients who said: "We understand that you're thinking of hiring Ms. Martin. Don't — or if you do, don't let her anywhere near our premises because she won't be allowed in". So the producer said: "What on earth is wrong with Jan Martin? She seems a very competent film-maker". And of course they said "Well, we can't really tell you. It's a very, very hush-hush secret. But we can give you a clue; we have heard from Scotland Yard that she has a very dubious background — something to do with terrorism".

So what the producer did was to immediately pass this on to Jan Martin. What he and the industrial client didn't know was that Jan's father was a recently retired Scotland Yard police officer, who did what retired Scotland Yard police officers are not supposed to do, he rang up a mate at Scotland Yard and said "Just find out what your records, your computer, have on my daughter, because they're accusing her of being a terrorist".

So his mate said "I'll do you a favour", and found out that when Jan and her husband had been on a driving holiday on the continent, and had been coming back exhausted after a long drive through Holland, they had stopped off at a cafe for a cup of tea before they got on the ferry. The cafe owner had looked at Jan's husband, thought he looked rather like the Baader-Meinhoff suspect whose pictures had been all over Dutch TV the previous night, and rang the local police saying "The man you want for that bombing attack is sitting in my cafe". The police didn't take any notice of this because they'd already caught the person they wanted. But, they noted the sighting and the identification of this alleged terrorist, and possibly passed it on to Interpol — we don't know — who passed it back to Scotland Yard and, presumably via the Special Branch, or perhaps via a friendly contact — again we don't know — it was passed on to this industrial client, who then tried to block Jan Martin's employment.

Now if I'd made this up you'd quite rightly say "That's ridiculous, it could never happen". But it did happen. It happened to a woman and her husband who have no connection with any terrorist organisation, no criminal record whatsoever, and a completely blameless employment record. And it was only because of the extraordinary coincidence that Jan Martin's father was a former police officer that they actually found out what had happened. So there you had secret information gethering, of information that was both inaccurate and irrelevant, that was not kept confidential to the only people, the police, who could justifiably have claimed any right to keep it.

Later in this session we will get a description of the basics of the Home Office scheme which has been put forward in the recent White Paper to deal with this sort of problem. First, there will be a Data Protection Registrar, an independent person who will have the responsibility of registering computer data banks holding personal information. Secondly, the law will incorporate principles of the new European Convention on Data Protection, namely that the information received should indeed be accurate, relevant and up-to-date, and that one should be able to make certain that that is indeed the case. And thirdly and perhaps most importantly, the White Paper proposes that data subjects should have a right of access to their own personal records. And that is perhaps the most crucial area in which the Home Office and the present government have got it right and the Lindop Committee got it wrong. The Lindop Committee did not propose data subjects grant of access, and the White Paper has done this and we welcome this.

Having said that, let me turn to what is wrong with the White Paper; and there;s quite a lot wrong with it. Essentially, the White Paper leaves out a very large number of the systems which cause the problems. The White Paper starts off (and the Minister keeps on repeating this), by saying that the real problem is computers; the threat to the individual's privacy comes from the scale on which computer technology makes it possible to hold personal information, and the speed by which that can be made available to people all across the country. Now it's quite true that computer technology changes the scale of the problem, but the basic problems I mentioned − wrong information, lack of confidentiality, etc. − are just as common, possibly even more common, amongst manual systems. Filing cabinets all across the country which hold records on every schoolchild in this country, every social work client in this country, scrappy bits of paper on every doctor's patient − most of the really sensitive information is not in fact kept on computer. There is no doubt that if we get a law which is restricted to computer data then most of the problems that people bring to organisations like the NCCL will not be dealt with at all.

And at the other end of the scale, even though the government say it's the size and the speed of the computer operations that they're worried about, they then go on to propose total exemption for some of the biggest and fastest computer systems in this country: that is to say, a blanket exemption from registration for national security systems, and some exemptions for any system dealing with law enforcement − and primarily of course police systems. The

White Paper is a little ragged round the edges, it simply says that
there will be "appropriate exemptions for data banks holding
information for law enforcement purposes". The Minister has been
in the business of rewriting the Paper subsequently saying "No, we
don't need to exempt police systems; they will be in the registration
system". But since the police do not want to be in the registration
system, and since the Minister has not specified which systems are
actually going to be exempt, we will be pushing very hard for no
exemptions whatsoever on the grounds that there shouldn't be any
systems whose very existence is secret.

A different question is which systems should be exempt from the
data subjects' access. And clearly no one in their right minds would
argue that, if the Inland Revenue were in the middle of a tax fraud
investigation, they should hand over the files to the suspect half way
through the investigation. But there's every reason why, for
instance, criminal conviction records should be open to the person
whom they purport to be about. Because over and over again, we
have people coming up in court on a fairly minor motoring offence
who, when they're asked "Have they got any form?" the police say
"Well, there was that conviction for sexual assault on a small boy",
and the man says "Excuse me, I never, I never"; but by the time he's
cottoned on to what's happened he's already been sentenced.
Criminal records are very often wrong; they appear in fact to have
got more inaccurate since the index of the system has been computerised. So people should be able to look at them and challenge their
accuracy.

The second thing that is wrong with the government's proposal
is the ommission of codes of practice. Lindop, quite rightly in our
view, proposed a series of detailed codes of practice which would
tell data users exactly what was expected of them. The White Paper
says we can have voluntary codes of practice (which we don't regard
as adequate), and also says that there will be regulations dealing
with the very sensitive data − medical data, criminal convictions,
that sort of thing. Regulations we assume means statutory instruments non-amendable by Parliament and drawn up by the Home
Office, not by the independent Data Protection Registrar, and we
want to change that as well.

Essentially, to summarise the system which we will be pressing
for and on which we're drafting our own Bill, we want the law to
cover manual as well as computerised systems, with the very
obvious exemption for one's own personal records − the government acknowledge that they will have to exempt the home computer enthusiast who keeps his address book on the computer, and
clearly amy system which deals with manual records will have to

exempt the manual address book. We endorse the proposals for the independent Registrar. We endorse the use of the Ruopean Convention principles. But we want to strengthen the right of access for the data subject by reducing the exemptions which are proposed in the White Paper. And we want to tighten up the remedies which are proposed in the White Paper so that if you know, or have reason to suspect, that information is being used about you in breach of the law on the Convention principles, then you can go to the Registrar who would have a big enough staff and sufficient powers to be able to investigate your complaint, and if necessary take action against the data user.

We hope that the government is going to come up with a Bill in the next Parliamentary session, which will almost certainly be the last Parliamentary session before the next election. If they don't we will have our own model Bill available and I hope that that will be taken on board by someone who comes up in the ballot for private member's Bills.

Let me end on this. We are not placing all our faith in legislation. Increasingly we are finding it possible to persuade local councils, employers, schools, education authorities, even police authorities, to adopt models of good practice for themselves, to adopt their own codes of practice on data protection and to come to organisations like NCCL to tell them what should go in those codes of practice. And I'd like to advertise, if I may, a book that we're about to publish called *Whose File is it Anyway?** whose author is Ruth Cohen of the National Consumers Council. What she has done is a study of different kinds of record-keeping systems − school, medical, employment − which are open to the data subject. And the conclusion we come to, which perhaps underlines the point Paul Sieghart started with, is that opening up your record-keeping systems to the individual who is concerned, respecting individual privacy, actually leads to a better quality of record-keeping systems and therefore, in the end, we will be actually improving the social administration of a very large part of welfare benefit, education, and so on by taking on board the issues of data protection and individual privacy.

* £2.25 from NCCL, 21 Tabard St, London SE1

A MEDICAL CASE HISTORY
DR. JOHN DAWSON

I'm speaking tonight for the British Medical Association, I represent the doctors. I thought it might be useful if I went back just very briefly to talk about the purpose of data protection as far as we're concerned. First of all, there is no gain that we can discern for *doctors* in data protection — we'd all much rather be getting on with something else. Data protection, as far as we're concerned, is for the *patient's* benefit. It is for the patient to decide what is confidential and what is not confidential. In the past there's been a tendency for people to say that family planning information, or history about venereal disease, is confidential because everyone knew it was confidential. Well, we may have thought that but we've changed — it is now for the patient to decide what is confidential and what is not. And the fact that I was a spotty adolescent with acne may be something that I feel very sensitive about, even though most people would regard it as being trivial. Similarly, if I have a hernia, an acute condition which can be cured with an operation, that may be something that many people would feel trivial and non-confidential information. But to someone whose firm is making redundancies and who may include you on the list of people in danger of being made redundant if they know you have a hernia (even though it's a curable, limited condition) that may be extremely sensitive information. Therefore, I stress, *patients* must decide about what is confidential information.

Let's balance that with the need to share information, both in terms of the community — for medical research — and also directly for the benefit of the patient by means of multi-disciplinary care, where if you want to give the best treatment that the NHS can you will probably need to involve therapists of various sorts — occupational therapists, physiotherapists, social workers and certainly other doctors.

We're quite clear that computers can provide security: we don't have any problem about that. At the same time, there is no doubt that computer systems would be insufficiently secure if someone can gain access, or allow someone else to run through records, drawing out records according to some criterion, then examining the whole record — for example finding a group of patients, chosen for instance on the basis of their religion. You can do that kind of thing very much more easily with a computer that you can by going through manual records, where — to take the old joke of doctors' handwriting — getting access to information is pretty difficult.

So let's talk about data protection now in terms of how the government proposals in the White Paper match up to what we require on behalf of our patients. First of all there is no mention of manual records in the White Paper – and this is unacceptable to us. We believe that there must be something in this data protection legislation on manual records for the simple pragmatic reason that for the foreseeable future the vast majority of records in the NHS are going to be held as manual records. Computers are being used in general practice and in hospitals to some extent; certain hospitals now have personal medical information held on quite large computers, and some GPs have age/sex registers with associated personal information held on small computers. But to my knowledge there are only about 200 computer systems in general practice out of 8000 surgeries and 26000 general practitioner principals, and there are probably a dozen major systems running in hospitals, with smaller systems elsewhere. We're talking about a very tiny proportion of the information used in the NHS. More to the point, there is no communication between the systems. So even though you may hold patients' records on a computer in your GP's surgery, if you want to transfer those notes to another GP because the patient has moved, or if you want to send a letter to hospital, you will have to print out what is held on the computer and send it as a paper record. Similarly in hospital, all pathology requests – that is requests for bio-chemistry, blood counts, special tests (especially those for venereal disease) – are in the form of human-readable requests, and the information will come back on paper. Discharge summaries from hospital to GPs, letters from consultants to other consultants or from consultants to community physicians, are all paper transactions. It is an absolute nonsense to say that a Bill, providing data protection only for computer held information, will have any impact on the NHS in the foreseeable future.

Now I've heard it said by government that if a Bill which applies to computer information becomes law, this will have a *moral* effect on the way in which manual records are held. Even the Home Office has difficulty keeping a straight face about that.

It is possible that you will see some changes. Let me mention bar codes – the things you see on cans and books and supermarket items. These are ways of describing information, and they are becoming very common. That means that the readers for them are becoming very common; you can produce bar codes with cheap printers. We could quite quickly make a transition to sending tightly-defined data around the place as bar codes, which would have a number of advantages in terms of transcribing information into smaller systems. But again, there is no significant gain there in terms of data protection. So far as we are concerned, you have got to have cover at least for the use that is made of the manually-held information in the NHS. Now people may gather information and that in itself is harmless. It is the *use* that you make of it that may damage somebody. So if you provide safeguards to limit the use that is made of it, that would go quite a long way to meeting our needs about manual records.

We have problems about the Registrar. The Registrar has to be independent and that we believe is achievable. What is not set out in the White Paper, are the duties the Registrar must have. The Registrar must have a positive duty to act during each year, and to report at the end of each year as to the action that he has carried out.

We have difficulties, among the medical lobby, with paragraph 17 of the White Paper – major difficulties. I'm not talking here about limiting access to medical records, which is mentioned I think implicitly in this paragraph. One of the things that the medical profession has had to change – in the sense of giving up – is the idea of an automatic denial of access to medical records. This is something about which the doctors are far more flexible than they were 5-10 years ago. What we do have a problem with is the sentence 'Registered data users who make information available to authorities in connection with (law enforcement) will not be required to register such disclosures of information'. That could mean that an administrator in a hospital could provide information to a police constable who wanted it, without having any requirement on that administrator to register that a disclosure of information had taken place. And that is not acceptable. The paragraph does not talk about a statutory right of access to information, but a person could choose to make information available to the police without registering, and that's not on. What I think we might be prepared to talk about is Parliament defining classes of crime for which access could then be requested or required by the police – so that, for example, if you're talking about a murder case then perhaps the police should have the right to follow up what they believe to be a serious lead by accessing data held in a medical information bank. But if they do that, it should be something that has been agreed by Parliament, because there is no further safeguard in this country. Then at least it's an open agreement, not a secret agreement between the police and the administrator, without the knowledge or consent of either the doctor or the patient. If that access is to be made under regulations defined by Parliament, then we would say that the fact of that access should be logged, and it should be published by the Regional Health Authority – the people who are responsible for the information bank – at some later time, possibly in an annual report. So you would be able see what use of information had been made under that rule or regulation.

We have agreed by now, I think, that there will be regulations for health information. Health information does get special treatment throughout the White Paper. This is because there is a general recognition now that people in this country want their personal medical information well treated. This is for the vast benefit of the NHS: if patients lose confidence in doctors, the NHS will slow down, because you have to repeat more tests and talk to people for longer if they won't tell you the truth. The cost goes up and it becomes more cumbersome than it is at the moment. We want regulations which will set out clearly the safeguards that there are for medical information. In summary, let me say again that we want all that on behalf of the patients. There is no gain in data protection for the doctors.

SOME POINTS OF LAW
RALPH SHUFFREY

I am responsible (amongst other things) for preparing a scheme for legislation on the lines of the Government White Paper. As Paul Sieghart indicated earlier on, the subject has a very long history, going back well beyond the Lindop Committee on which he and Charles Read were distinguished members. The Lindop Committee proposed, as indeed the last government indicated, that there should be a Data Protection Authority. But since the Lindop Committee reported, there has been a change of government, after the General Election in 1979. And there is a marked distaste on the part of the present government for anything in the nature of a Quango, as these bodies tend to be called, and a wish to produce a scheme for data protection that will be as simple as possible, placing the minimum burden on industry and on public funds. So we start with a desire to do the minimum that is necessary to protect personal data.

The Registrar will be the key figure in the government's proposals, and registration the key process. The object of registration will be to provide public information about the existence of computerised data systems holding personal data. As we see it, after the Bill becomes law, there would be a period of not more than a few months during which data users − other than those exempt for one reason or another − would be required to inform the Registrar, giving brief particulars of their system. They would not then have to wait to be licenced, or given approval, by the Registrar or his office.

They would be able to continue in business. In this way, the Registrar would building up a fairly comprehensive knowledge of the whole range of computer systems holding personal information and he would certainly, we would intend, report regularly to Parliament about the use of his powers, which, as indicated in the White Paper, are fairly extensive.

He would be enjoined by the Bill to have regard to what are set out in the European Convention as general principles. These principles, which we reproduced in the White Paper — such as 'Information shall be obtained and processed fairly and lawfully, shall be held for a specified and legitimate purpose' and so on — are for the most part vague and imprecise. We don't consider that a simple requirement on data users to comply with these principles would really be either sufficient protection for data subjects, or give the Courts a job they could reasonably undertake, or indeed give users much idea of what they were expected to do while complying with these principles. The principles need to be interpreted and elucidated.

The Lindop Committee would have done this through a series of Codes of Practice applying to various sectors. We did spend considerable time trying to work out how one could operate in that way, but we came to the conclusion that it would really be virtually impossible within any reasonable time-scale to divide up all computer operations into specific sectors. There would be enormous problems of definition, and by the time one had issued Codes of Practice comprehensively covering each sector, many years would have elapsed. Our view rather is that general guidance is needed on these principles, directed to the Registrar, and embodied we think *in* the statute so that they would be amendable by Parliament and of course there for users to see.

The sort of guidance on has in mind is that the Registrar should consider how a data subject might be *harmed* if information had been processed *un*fairly. Were things done in such a way that the data subject wouldn't have expected that to happen when he provided this information about himself? A fair amount of general guidance of this sort, we believe, will probably be necessary in the Bill. There is no reason at all why any particular sector shouldn't produce, with the help of the Registrar, its own Code of Guidance, but we wouldn't wish to hold up the implementation of the Bill while every area is covered by its particular Code.

Now the remedies for the data subject. There will of course be certain criminal offences, which are already referred to in the White Paper. It will be a criminal offence, after a certain period has elapsed, to operate unregistered; to fail to comply with notices issued by the Registrar (because the Registrar will have power to issue notices to data users requiring them to amend their systems); or to make a false statement to the Registrar; or refuse him access to computer systems/or documents. Again, it will be an offence to disclose data to persons other than those listed on the registration details. Also, there will need to be certain additions to the civil law, to deal for example with where a data subject may be harmed through the use of inaccurate data, or as a result of the data user's inadequate security measure.

All this is subject to there being certain exempt areas. Reference has been made to paragraph 17 of the White Paper where we refer specifically to exemptions on the grounds of national security. And I'm afraid there must always be things in the security area of which there is no public knowledge. As for the police, much of the information they hold in computers is purely factual, relating for example to people's past convictions. It's certainly not the case that the bulk of these records will be excluded from the Bill. We would expect the bulk of all these, for example on the Police National

Computer at Hendon, to be registered and most of it made accessible – consisting, as it mostly does, of factual data, for example, on vehicle owners or indices of people's previous convictions.

On medical data, I'm in entire argrement with most of what Dr. Dawson has just said – except, I think, the example he gave about the passing of information to the police by a hospital administrator with reference to this sentence in paragraph 17, where he said 'Registered data users who make information available to the authorities in connection with (law enforcement) will not be required to register such disclosures of information'. In other words, if that takes place at the moment, and to disclose it would prejudice the efforts of the law enforcement authorities to obtain a conviction, or whatever, it wouldn't be registered and certainly not

disclosed to the public. But it's very difficult to be specific about a particular instance, I think a lot of these things will only be tested when we have a Bill, when we have a Registrar, when someone challenges what has taken place and it's put to the test. It is almost impossible in a Bill setting up general machinery to legislate in such a way as to draw a hard and fast line between what may happen and what may not happen.

We were praised by Patricia Hewitt for saying (as we had to because of a provision in the European Convention) that data subjects should normally have access to data about them, and the

Lindop Committee were by implication blamed for not recommending that. But this is an extremely difficult area. It partly depends on what you mean by 'personal data,' and it's only when you begin to get down to drafting the provisions of a Bill that you realise that it's not just a matter of saying, 'Well, this applies to all the domains of personal data, full stop'. On our reckoning, there are at least three different levels of personal data. There are the factual things about me such as my weight, my height, my age, which are clearly covered. Then there are what one would call 'judgemental data'. If in the Civil Service someone has marked me as having performed well or badly – we have a scale of 1 to 6 in Civil Services Reports – that is a pretty solid piece of judgemental data in an annual performance report, which is incidentally accessible to Civil Servants if they want it. So one has factual assessment, weight and so on; and judgemental assessment. But thirdly we have things like the Management Plan that in 1990 they may move Mr. X to take charge of that division in Bahrein or somewhere, and move so-and-so back. Perhaps rather tentative plans about people. How much of that, which is often called 'control data,' is to be accessible? The Institute of Personnel Management for one are very concerned about this. And it's when you get down to things like that that you begin to realise what a problem access is, and it's not just a matter of saying that it's a good thing for everybody to have access. It can cause quite a few problems, as can the definition of automatic processing.

Well, you might say, 'why not include the lot, manual data as well?' My opinion is that if manual data were included in this Bill that would sink it, and it would never get though, because of the additional administrative costs. It may be unfair, but it's rather like having a Bill about motor traffic which you can't get though because of an amendment to include bicycles.

The Mass Media: Diversity or Standardization?

The introduction of satellite and cable TV, video cassettes etc. offer the opportunity for greater diversity of information, education and ideas; it also brings the danger of mass propaganda. Will the proliferation of choice lead to the fragmentation of society and likelihood of social unrest? The country could be consulted on any issue at the push of a button, but will everyone have buttons to push? And what does this mean in terms of agenda setting and the collective nature of political activity? How will IT affect culture? It should be technically possible to give more air time to minority and non-establishment views, but will the power remain where the money is, with the multi-nationals and the Hollywood ethic? Many countries are calling for international agreements to control satellite broadcasts from other nations. Is it possible to encourage links between similar interest groups in different nations while resisting 'cultural aggression'? And what does this mean for increased cooperation East/West, North/South?

Chairman: Peter Large, Speakers: John Howkins, Brenda Maddox, Stuart Hood.

THE NEW COMMUNICATIONS MATRIX

As IT advances, one of the things it is starting to change is the *pattern* of communication channels. Back in the steam age, there was a single 2 x 2 x 1 matrix: human verbal communication could be either in the spoken or the written *form,* and either in the one-to-one or the one-to-many *mode,* but always as a two-way *flow.* You could either write a letter or a newspaper article, and you could talk either to a friend or to a public meeting. And the receivers of your message could generally answer back. To that, the telegraph only added speed for letters, and the telephone reduced distance, so turning many slow exchanges of letters into quick conversations.

The advent of wire*less* telegraphy introduced some profound changes in that pattern: the one could now communicate with more of the many at a time, who no longer had to go to the Town Hall to listen. Nor could they heckle: the two-way flow had, in this instance, been cut down to one (and that has only recently, and partially, been restored by the phone-in programme). And this change affected not only the verbal form of communication, but its musical one also. Then the cinema added a new form — moving pictures — but still in the one-to-one mode, and as a one-way flow.

TV combined what both radio and the cinema could do, but the visual impact of moving pictures in the home had a remarkable effect. The portrayal of events in distant places in 'real time' — that is, as those events actually happen — has led to a great shrinking of the planet, now that we can see for ourselves how others live, and what they think and say and do. That has revolutionised perceptions, attitudes — and, most important, expectation — all over the world.

But radio and TV are both mass media: at any given time, they are limited to a one-way flow in the one-to-many mode. Until recently, the only communication channel that could function in the 'some-to-some' mode, where the transmitters can (within limits) choose their receivers, and the receivers can choose their transmitters within the same channel, has been print: newspapers, periodicals, and books. Print has another unique feature: it is a permanent medium in time, unlike radio and TV which are fleeting ones (unless, now, you record them on tape). If you miss an item in the middle of a news bulletin, or a vital sentence in a talk, you can't go back to it. In print, you can; and you can also decide at what speed and in what order you will read different items; go back to them at any time; look them up when you need them; cross reference them; make notes about them; discover new connexions between them, and so forth. Print leaves you free to choose your own tempo and rhythm. But print, like broadcasting, only functions as a one-way flow: it mediates monologue, not dialogue.

IT is now opening up a whole new range of possibilities — in forms, modes, flows and all their combinations. For instance, the technology already exists for the home printer (sometimes called Telefax), on which you can order the news pages from the *Daily Telegraph*, the arts pages from the *Financial Times*, the letters page from *The Times*, page 3 of the *Sun*, and the editorials and features from the *Guardian*, all before you go to bed, to find them waiting for you at breakfast — not even on paper, but on re-useable plastic. Then there is Teletext, or Teledata, or Viewdata, or Videotext: the nomenclature hasn't settled down yet. Ceefax and Oracle are becoming familiar, but these are still 'broadcast' in the one-to-many mode as a one-way flow. Prestel functions in a new some-to-many mode, and is pioneering 'narrowcasting' as a new some-to-some system with its 'closed user groups', so paralleling in the form of print what cable TV will mediate in the form of moving pictures. Perhaps most important of all, many of these new systems will be 'interactive', that is two-way: the receiver will be able to answer back to the transmitter. Electronic dialogue and polylogue will become possible, and even commonplace.

So the old 2 x 2 x 1 matrix is expanding fast: it's already at least 3 x 4 x 2 (that is, six times bigger), and it's still growing.

Some Problems

All this will raise a great many problems – over content, over access (both for transmitters and receivers) and therefore over control. Some of those problems (but by no means all) were addressed by the contributors to this session.

John Howkins provides a thoughtful overview, raising far more questions that anyone could answer, and showing how fragmented (and typically pragmatic) the UK decision-making machinery still is in this area. There is a vast amount of work to be done here, and hardly anyone has yet started to do it. Eventually, there will have to be a substantial body of integrated information law, based on a fundamental 'right to communicate', with the attendant allocation of all the correlative duties, responsibilities and accountability. It is no longer just a question of being free to say what one wants to say: people who have things to say aslo need to participate in making the policies about communication channels which will enable others to *hear* what they have to say – and people who want to listen will likewise need to make sure that they can hear what is being said. (I recall my six-year-old daughter once asking me why I could get on TV to say things she didn't think were particularly important (human rights, I think it was), while no one ever asked *her* to broadcast all the important things she wanted to get across to the world (the foolishness of schooling, I think it was).I've been wondering ever since what the answer to that question is.)

Brenda Maddox confines her contribution to the single area of cable TV. What she recounts is illuminating, and not only for that new medium among the many there are to come. There is no technical reason, for instance, why satellite TV should always be distributed by cable: individual dish aerials on people's own roofs could receive it direct. But that will then raise the spectre of 'culture pollution': the Canadian public authorities are already complaining that their population is being submerged in values which US TV beams across their border; so, for different reasons, are the East German authorities about what the West transmits. The Danes (much like the Welsh) are starting to worry that Swedish TV will eventually erode their own language. How would the Ayatollah

Khomeini respond if Iranian villagers could see the Western permissive society on their TV screens? The UN Committee on the Peaceful Uses of Outer Space is supposed to be working on this. Predictably, it hasn't got very far: its last suggestion was that a government whose people could receive foreign satellite broadcasts without that government's consent would be remitted to its right of reprisal under international law – which presumably means shooting down the offending satellite!

So which is to be: the free flow of information across national borders, or the right of every people to preserve its cultural identity? It doesn't look as if you can have both.

Radical dissent

Finally, Stuart Hood raises some challenging questions. The radical, he says, wants *real* freedom of communication – not just in broadcasting, which can only ever purvey the 'Parliamentary consensus' from which he dissents, but in the new forms of narrowcasting, in which all sorts of dissenting views could be heard – such as those of Brixton blacks about police methods in their area.

So far, so good. But then comes the test question: should racists and sexists also be allowed to put *their* views across over these new channels? Hood seems to think not – apparently on the grounds that 'absolute freedom is not something which we can hope to experience or obtain'. May be so: the tolerant have always had to face the paradox of how to tolerate the intolerant. But in that case, why absolute freedom for the Brixton blacks, and censorship for the Brixton branch of the National Front, when neither of them reflects the Parliamentary consensus? Surely not just because the views of the first are more fashionable, or more attractive, or more rational, or kinder, or more easy to justify – let alone because they are more palatable to Hood's radicals. As the European Court of Human Rights said in the *Little Red Schoolbook* case, freedom of expression 'applies not only to information and ideas that are favourably received or regarded as inoffensive or as a matter of indifference, but also to those that offend, shock or disturb the State or any sector of the population'. Which is surely the radical critic's whole point.

Hood says that 'No society is conceivable which does not set limits of one type or another to what may be said or discussed'. If that is so – and I personally would not agree that no such society is 'conceivable' – then it is *society* which has to set the limits for everyone, and that is precisely what we now do through the 'Parliamentary consensus'. Once you challenge that, in order to be able to dissent from it, then you cannot stop others doing the same, however much they may dissent from *your* views – unless, of course, you manage to overthrow the whole system which produces the Parliamentary consensus in the first place, and put yourself and your like-minded friends in its place. In the countries where that has happened – and they make a sad tally in today's world – the prospects of later radical dissenters from *that* consensus ever again making themselves heard – outside their prison cells, that is – are usually pretty remote.

Electronic referenda

Hood is the only contributor to discuss the possibilities of future instant electronic referenda, which could soon become technically quite feasible through interactive cable systems. But he does not seem to like them: to him, they would be 'the application of the process of privatisation to the political process'. Worse (and more simply), they would be 'the suppression of participation' – apparently because he believes that the voters' judgements would simply reflect the views presented to them by the media, lapped up uncritically within 'the cellular family'. That seems to display a massive contempt for the ability of the ordinary citizen to have a mind of his or her own, and a remarkable arrogance about the power of broadcasters. (He should try watching a few TV programmes in a pub, and hear the scathing comments of the audience.) One can only hope that his attitudes on this question are not typical of his professional colleagues' – otherwise we would have serious cause to worry about our own broadcasting media, and the effects that working for them has on their senior executives.

There are other problems with instant electronic referenda, which are rather different from Hood's fantasy. One is again the problem of 'dissonant time horizons'. Suppose one day a government decides to hold an instant electronic referendum to find out what the electorate thinks of the new plans for expanding the nuclear power programme. And suppose, just at that time, the Third Gulf War is in full swing, and oil has just gone up to $100 a barrel. That government might well get 70% support.

Suppose now it's five years later, the contracts have all been placed, the foundations have been poured, the steelwork is going up, and thousands are busy fabricating the reactors, the boilers and the turbines. Now things are quiet in the Gulf, and oil is back to $50 a barrel. Just then, someone decides to have another electronic referendum – but the day before it takes place, the Seven League Island reactor incident hits the TV screens. What happens if 60% now vote to cancel the programme, at a cost of hundreds of millions of pounds and tens of thousands of jobs?

Most people, most of the time, only have to make decisions for the short, or the medium-short, term. Decisions which can profoundly affect the future of a whole nation need to be taken with much longer time horizons. Unlike the decisions taken by individual businesses, these cannot afford to be seriously wrong. A business can founder without too much pain, and can be replaced: a nation can not. Perhaps that is the best argument for representative — rather than direct — democracy, and even for a permanent (and inherently unaccountable) civil service. So long, that is, as *someone* is accountable to the public for what it does — and that is the main justification for having professional politicians.

The Third World again

Hood is also the only one who mentions the problems of the Third World in this area. Some of these are still of a quite different order from ours: having even a postal system that works reliably, let alone a telephone in every rural village. (A TV set would need an electricity supply.) Besides, they find themselves exclusively at the receiving end of communication by the mass media: when did you last see a TV programme about the Republic of Mali, made by Malians and telling you not only how they see themselves, but how they see *you*? That was the burden of the MacBride Report which Hood mentions, and which proposed a New World Information and Communication Order.

Like the New International Economic Order, I suspect that too will be a long time coming.
Paul Sieghart

COMMUNICATIONS POLICY &
CULTURAL CONTEXT
JOHN HOWKINS

To summarise the political and cultural context of information technology and communication technology is probably harder in the middle of 1982, in the middle of Information Technology Year, than at any time for many years. The sudden focus on information technology, quite properly, has raised questions and revealed problems rather than provided answers. Some people even find it strange that 'information' is a matter of social concern and government policy. Communications policy, of course, has existed for some years, although more often in its constituent parts (TV, telephones, films, newspapers) than as a coherent set. But communications policy, too, is now changing out of recognition. The situation in broadcasting, film, the press is certainly more complicated now than it was in the last great shift, in 1955, when broadcast advertising was legalised. It is more complicated than it was in 1945, when television began. Perhaps better analogies are with the second half of the 19th century; when wired and then wireless telegraphy were invented. But the differences are more striking than the similarities, not least in the degree of government intervention, and the timescale of innovation and investment.

Each technical innovation has been made and shaped by people who, with few exceptions, were outside the existing communications infrastructure. Telegraphy and broadcasting began when engineers and scientists and speculators joined together to push the new systems into the mainstream of society. This entrepreneurial adventurism lapsed in the 1920s, but reappeared in the 1950s when ITV was launched by people who until then had had few opportunities to operate mainstream communication systems. During Information Technology Year 1982, as the pressure mounts for the government to authorise private cable pay-TV systems, a similar sea change can be observed. People who have been prevented by regulation or the costs of entry from operating telephone, press or broadcasting facilities are now realising that they might have a chance to operate a cable service and thus provide a hybrid of all three of these services.

The change is threefold. First, an apparently endless stream of gadgets and devices has been developed and marketed and in most cases eagerly bought. These new gadgets are 'information technology', and remain the focus of most UK policy. But there is a wider context. In 1970 the Japanese predicted the emergence of the 'information society' where most people would spend their time and earn their living by dealing in information. The Japanese forecast tremendous changes in the collection, processing and distribution of information; not just snazzier hi-fi units, but in computerisation and telecommunications. The Japanese were especially eager to identify this new trend because they have no oil or energy reserves, and are dependent on the processing of imported materials for economic survival. By the mid-1970s Japan's predictions were confirmed when the USA became the first country in which more than half the workforce could be classed as being in the information sector. During the 1980s, it is expected, practically all other members of the Organisation of Economic Cooperation and Development (OECD) will follow suit. The evidence surrounds us: from the shortage (and unattractive returns) of investment in British Leyland, compared with the money now being poured into computers and office equipment, and the rash of new video shops. There is another, third context, perceived as yet only dimly. We do not yet really understand what information is, or how it works. Even the comparatively straightforward and visible forms of the mass media elude definition and comprehension; how much longer will we have to wait for an understanding of information and communication in all their forms, so that they can claim an intellectual and academic standing and basis for policy making?

The potential is vast. It is increasingly recognised that 'information' is the medium of change at all levels of organisation, from the biological to the social. But in all OECD countries except perhaps Japan there is no real recognition of this holistic approach by government. In the UK, there is no collaboration between policies on transport and policies on telecommunications; and there is no consultation (except in one temporary Cabinet Office subcommittee) between the Department of Education and Science and the other government Departments with responsibility for information and communications.

In spite of the interlocking complexities of this change, I want to try to list very briefly some points that seem important. They are all what I would call political or social factors. I will leave technology aside for the moment.

First, the uncertainty about the nature of information itself precludes agreement over its meaning and importance, and favours a pragmatic approach to change. For something so essential to the proper functioning of every organism and every organisation, both information and communication have remained remarkably irreducible by theory and argument. At the most basic level, information can be seen in two perspectives: as a resource, (in some sense, a public resource); and as a commodity. Some knowledge is treated as a resource in one context (eg academic centres) and as a commodity in others (eg commercial companies). The way in which society treats information will affect its attitude to the split between the information-rich and the information-poor. Communication has also eluded a generally agreed definition. The mathematical theory of linear cause and effect, still assumed in most academic work, is increasingly unsatisfactory. But the systems-based, holistic, ecological alternatives are incomplete. How can one regulate something which one doesn't understand? Public service broadcasting worked because Reith had a precise vision of its imperatives. Who will stand up for public service telecommunications?

The second point is the timescale of the change in information and communication. The emergence of the information society has been compared to several earlier great shifts in social organisation. But these earlier changes took place over many generations. Even the Industrial Revolution spanned many decades (can you imagine

Industrial Revolution *Year* as we now have Information Technology Year?). The Japanese were the first to realise what was happening; but few people listened. As recently as 1974 the Annan Committee was unaware of the possibility of a sudden change in direction. Its report said that 'eventually government will have to face the problem of communication'; but not, presumably, in the 15 years with which Annan was concerned. It said only that 'there may have to be changes in the constitutional arrangements for broadcasting by the end of the century'.

Suddenly, the place increased. Constitutional arrangements are now being studied by Lord Hunt (who must wish that Lord Annan had had the gift of better foresight). Pay-TV, which did not exist in the USA when Annan was working, now has 15 million subscribers, and is the favourite for legislation in the UK. Satellites, which Annan virtually ignored, are now being built. And whereas the fourth channel took 11 years to be allocated, the Home Secretary gave two satellite TV channels to the BBC without any whisper of a public debate. Incidentally, the haste with which the new is being licensed, compared to the old, has upset some hard-won public benefits. When the IBA advertised for applicants for the ITV licences it encouraged newcomers to apply; when the Home Office was considering licences for the pilot pay-TV projects it declared that because of the shortness of time it could hear applications only from existing licensees.

The third point, which makes contemporary change unique, is that society is utterly different both in itself and in relation to the innovation. Society is much more complex than in the 19th century;

and as it becomes based on computer telecommunications it becomes much more vulnerable. It is extremely vulnerable to almost every form of human weakness, from terrorism to theft to incompetence. In London the IRA attack soldiers on ceremonial duties; future terrorists will do more damage if they strike not at harmless ceremony but at the computerised infrastructure of banking, industry and retailing. A modern society is very vulnerable to an interruption to its telephone system, its computerised payrolls and its computerised traffic systems.

The fourth factor is the real recession that is spreading through all OECD countries and from which we look unlikely to recover for many years. How, in recession, do we pay for the new services? Not only how do we pay for the investment (the main concern of the present government) but also how does the user pay? An increase in the gap between the information-rich and the information-poor is probably inevitable; certainly, there will be an increase in our awareness of that gap.

Tied to this social change, fifth, is the increase in productivity in the service sector. Agriculture is highly automated and productivity rates have been very high for twenty or thirty years. Most manufacturing industries achieved high productivity on the factory floor ten or twenty years ago. Offices, hitherto the least efficient, are now also recognising the need for increased productivity. One element of this is the flood of new office equipment. This new productivity threatens the number of jobs. According to a report by the European Trade Union Institute, *negotiating Change,* completed in August 1982 (*The Times,* 16 August 1982) even the so-called 'expanding industries of electronics and information technology' lost 65,000 jobs in the five years to April 1982. The workforce that has moved from the land to the factory, and then into the office, is running out of places to go. This relationship of work to reward, and of paid activities to unpaid activities, is probably the most fundamental change of the next twenty years.

Sixth, information will have an increasing effect on international relations. One of the most cherished principles of Western society is the supremacy of the nation state in world affairs. Another is the principle of the free flow of information. In an interdependent, international, information society these two axions are increasingly in contradiction. In Canada, the free flow of data between Canada and the USA has meant that Canadian government agencies, banks and commercial companies are becoming excessively dependent on data that is stored and processed in the USA. As much as 90% of the flow of data between Canada and the USA is internal, non-market data being sent from a Canadian subsidiary to its US headquarters.

The Canadian company is thus brought under the control of US regulation: the Canadian information is not subject to the Canadian government in Ottawa but to the US government in Washington. As information becomes the chief wealth of a society, so the society may find its wealth being stored elsewhere and regulated by foreign governments. Gold ingots can be locked away. Data, especially private data, are more elusive.

Seventh, many new techniques not only do something better (or faster, or more cheaply) but they transform the perceptions and activities of the operator. A word processor is usually seen as a clever typewriter (and is usually sold as such). But after a few weeks the user of a word processor begins to gain an entirely new understanding of his work; the technology actually stimulates a transformation of his ways of working, and therefore of his ways of earning money and spending time. A cordless telephone can create new relationships between home and office which extend beyond the ability simply to make and receive telephone calls in new places. Business satellite services transform the relationship of city centre and suburb and town; and can do so continually without requiring men to cut down trees for telephone poles and string wires across fields.

Eighth, the government's influence over the developments of information technology is very pervasive. In most Western societies, publishing, the press, cinema and even broadcasting have remained outside direct government control. With print, especially, people have been very free to print and distribute and read. This freedom has usually been judged by political criteria; but it also has moral, intellectual, and sexual parameters. Whether someone bought and read something printed; whether or not they exercised the myriad opportunities to communicate and travel; these decisions were private. Increasingly they are becoming a matter of public policy.

In Europe the 'information revolution' is a revolution launched and steered by government. The chief protagonists have been the French government of Valéry Giscard d'Estaing, and the UK government of Margaret Thatcher. During 1982 both Thatcher and François Mitterand, Giscard's successor, have moved along strongly similar lines (which gives the lie to rumours that it's all a Tory plot – or a Socialist one).

It is noticeable, incidentally, that in this country neither the Labour Party nor the SDP have generated much of a policy on information technology (debates on IT in the House of Commons have attracted few MPs). The Labour Party's thinking is still locked into the reform of the mass media. The SDP case is different. There is an interesting hypothesis that while the Tories were the party of land and the agricultural sector, and while the Labour Party was born on the factory floor, the SDP are the party of the professions and services; the party, indeed, of the information society. Some half-recognition of this fundamental linkage can be seen in the criticisms that the SDP is a creation of the 'media'. Intended as a rebuke, the sneer contains a grain of truth. Fifty years ago, many people attacked the Labour Party for being the creation of the trade unions.

The government's extensive intervention in information technology is not the result of any clear policy towards information technology. The decision to convert British Telecom into British Telecom PLC, and to sell half the shares in the new company to the public, is not based on any agreement about the best way to own and operate a national telecommunication network; and certainly not on any calculation about the proper balance between telecommunications as a commercial offering and telecommunications as a welfare service.

This confusion is evident in the crossed lines in Westminster and Whitehall whenever policies on information and communications are discussed. The Department of Trade is responsible for publishing and the film industry; the Department of Industry is responsible for the aerospace industry (including satellites) and British Telecom; the Home Office is responsible for broadcasting, cable systems − and data protection. This allocation of responsibilities which, like Topsy, has 'simply growed and growed' is unsuitable to prepare policies for the next few years. A less anachronistic arrangement is now being sought by four cabinet committees, the Information Technology Advisory Panel and the Hunt Committee.

When Britain committed £70 million to the European experiment in satellite broadcasting, the announcement was made not by the Home Office but by the Department of Industry (incidentally, the scale of the new business compared to the old can be gauged from that figure of £70 million, which is more than twice the amount the National Film Finance Corporation has disbursed since its foundation in 1950). The Department of Industry has become the lead agency in the promotion and financing of the new information technologies, although when these matters are discussed in Cabinet the Secretaries of State for the Home Office and the Department of Trade maintain a strong voice. This shift in departmental responsibilities may undercut the authority of the Hunt committee. In cabinet discussions this autumn the Home Office will be presenting the Hunt committee's report, while the Department of Industry will be presenting the proposals of the commercial companies who want to construct and operate cable systems.

In this confused scene, the people with the clearest priorities are those who expect to manufacture and sell the new technologies. For others, the future is very unclear. The social, cultural and intellectual arguments are very confused, especially to companies who have grown up in different media (the press, broadcasting, film). How do we know what's important? In retrospect, the most significant event of the last few years may have been the BBC's insistence that its new licence allow the corporation to engage in satellite broadcasting and cable transmission to specialised audiences; conversely, the IBA's failure to have its regulatory structure altered accordingly may be more important than its 'franchise affair' and the appointment of ITV companies for the next ten years. How do we know what's important? How do we champion what's important?

There is another quandary. How can we reconcile the recognition that communication is the defining characteristic of human society, of human organisation, with the need to keep it democratic? How can we being communication into the spotlight without giving the means of communication to the highest bidder? How can we stop telecommunications, the new highways, from being taken over by juggernauts? How can we ensure that an 'information society' is also a society of wisdom, knowledge and care?

THE RISE AND RISE OF CABLE
BRENDA MADDOX

The truism that advances in technology take public policy unpre-
pared, does not apply to cable television. Few technical developments have been so analysed in their formative years as has cable.
Few have been so restrained by government policies designed to
make them grow only in a predetermined, socially useful pattern.
Probably none has so confounded predictions and seen the original
policies controlling it so totally reversed.

In the early 1970s, cable television − which brings television into
homes by coaxial cable rather than an aerial on the roof − seemed
the perfect technology for catching in the bud. The faith placed in it
in the United States by economic and social planners was, according
to one observer at the time, "almost religious: it begins with something that was once despised − a crude, makeshift way of bringing
television into remote areas − and sees it transformed over the
opposition of powerful enemies into the cure for the ills of modern
urban American society".

In the United States, cable television had emerged in rural areas
as a spontaneous and unexpected by-product of a decision by the
Federal Communications Commission. In 1952, the FCC had
chosen to allocate television stations around the country according
to a policy of "localism". Each television station was intended (as
were radio stations a generation earlier, when they were first allocated) to serve as a mouthpiece for the community. Each station
was also expected to use the local audience as its financial base
through selling advertising. This policy created a national patch-
work: urban areas with television, and large stretches in between
without it. About 30% of the American population had a poor
television signal or none at all. In consequence, rural television
dealers, anxious to sell sets, rigged up tall masts and caught television signals floating through the air from city stations. They piped
the signals over cables into people's homes. Subscribers to the
service paid a monthly fee.

It was soon obvious that the picture delivered by cable was of a
far higher quality than that obtained through a domestic aerial. As
the years went by, two other advantages became apparent. Both
arose from the great bandwidth of the coaxial cable (300 megaherz,
compared to the 5 megaherz of an ordinary telephone line). One
advantage was that cable could deliver a great many more television
programmes than could be received with a rooftop aerial. The other
was that it could carry signals in both directions.

The possibility of extra television channels caught the imagination of social planners. It opened up the opportunity for truly local television, as well as what the Sloan Commission on Cable Communications in 1971 called "the television of abundance" — channels for minorities, for education, for local government, for public access. Even more socially useful possibilities were foreseen in the two-way, or interactive, capability of the cable. It could allow the viewer to vote, shop or respond to questions from home. These possibilities were well researched by the Rand Corporation in a series of optimistic papers. Rand predicted the day of the Wired Ghetto, when the poor would receive health information and job advice on their television sets.

The American broadcasting industry was swift to perceive the threat in cable's multi-channel capacity. It could siphon away audiences for local television by filling the extra channels with a wider variety of fare than was available over the airwaves. It could include programmes snatched from distant television stations. It could also offer "pay television" — special channels of sports events or films for a special fee. The broadcasting industry accordingly began a campaign to restrict what cable systems might show. It went under the banner: "Save free TV".

That is just where we are in Britain today. In 1977, the Annan Committee, set up by the government to study the future of broadcasting, concluded that a national information network based on cable TV was both inevitable and desirable. But it added: "In delay there is hope". Annan advocated waiting until the turn of the century, when control of cable TV could be invested in a single publicly-accountable authority which would pay for the network's construction out of public funds. In the meantime, cable should be allowed to develop (i.e. offer more television programmes than could be received over the air) only as a local community television service. Five years later, at the time of writing, another committee, under Lord Hunt, is already investigating how public service broadcasting can be protected when Britain is wired for 24 or more channels of cable television.

But why should a government protect one kind of video delivery system to the detriment of another? That was the question which was unanswerable in America during the late 1970s. It led to the dismantling of the rules holding back cable television. The rules were suddenly seen as simply protecting an existing industry, dominated by three rich networks, against a newcomer.

The question put in Britain, however, is easy to answer. What we have is too good to be jeopardised lightly: "more" may in truth be "less". Britain has a unique tradition of broadcasting that is totally contrary to the American one. The preservation of standards has, since 1922, been accepted as a responsibility of government. So, too, is the goal of universal reception of signals of good quality. Talk of "deregulation" in Britain, therefore, has to be seen against these two conflicting facts: the push of technology, and the desire to uphold the traditions of the past.

It also needs to be understood that there are two kinds of deregulation in broadcasting: of access and of content. And it can be applied to some media more easily than others. In American broadcasting, three different media have been touched by deregulation: radio, television, and cable television (now officially recognised as non-broadcasting); and a fourth – satellite broadcasting – may be drawn in as well. But deregulation does not mean that no rules remain.

Radio has been deregulated as to its content. Stations no longer have to limit the amount of advertising to broadcast programmes that are in the public interest, to keep records of their output, or to maintain balance. That is the extent of deregulation. The FCC still controls entry to radio. A station may not broadcast without a licence, and the FCC retains the right to take the licence away.

Television is still strictly controlled, in terms of entry, programme balance and amount of advertising. The new chairman of the FCC would like to deregulate television, as has been done with radio. As there are almost as many television outlets as newspapers, what is the justification for requiring television to mute its editorial voice and present all sides of an argument, while letting newspapers be partisan? That, anyway, is the argument. A beginning of television regulation awaits in Low-Powered Television – new, cheap, short-range television stations which the FCC plans to licence.

Cable television is the object lesson for deregulation. There was once a philosophy at the FCC called "creative regulation" – making lots of rules so that a new technology would grow in the public interest. Cable bore the full brunt. Now almost all the rules have been thrown out – some by the courts. Forcing cable to show only old movies, for example, was declared to infringe freedom of the press. Now operators do not have to provide local access for citizens or to originate programmes. They may carry advertising. The FCC is dismantling its Cable Television Bureau. But city governments, who have the power to give local franchises to cable companies, are often reinstating these demands themselves. Deregulation of cable often just means regulation at a lower level of government.

So far, the American rule that persists most conspicuously is the one that British cable operators want removed first: the 'must-carry' rule. A cable system must carry all local television signals that have significant local audiences. It cannot fill up all its channels (and 12 is still the capacity of the average system) with out-of-town or Home Box Office pay-TV signals.

Deregulation in British terms will probably mean simply that the Home Office loosened some of its grip on cable programming. Otherwise, despite the government's wildly enthusiastic plans for cable television, trusteeship is almost certainly the principle that will stay. This will be true because the government's certain to ignore the main point − that cable is "narrowcasting", not broadcasting. Rules made for broadcasting are not appropriate to cable and it could be allowed the freedom to offer the public a variety of specialised choices and see what it wants to buy. The British cable industry does not dare to argue so boldly on its own behalf. It knows that cable has a dirty-movie image, so it is offering a kind of self-policing Cable Council to guard the standards of what is shown on cable and to reassure Mrs Mary Whitehouse. But perhaps the government will set up its own Cable Council. Even that would be preferable to the Home Offive monitoring the programme schedules of the cable companies − a kind of stealthy censorship.

For my part, I am glad that some form of regulation will continue, heavy-handed though it will be. There is no way that the number of channels in Britain − by satellite or by cable − can be increased without jeopardising the quality of the BBC and ITV. Anything that fragments audiences must weaken the financial base of either − the licence fee or the regional advertising monopoly.

But the tide is unstoppable. The multi-channels are coming. The challenge is to minimise the risk. One way is to ensure that the national services are represented on the new channels. Mr Whitelaw has seen to that by giving the BBC both satellite channels to start with. He should now insist on a must-carry rule, even if there has to be a special dispensation for places like Wales where old, four-channel systems would be saturated with the national services, leaving no room for pay-TV and other cable fillers.

The British cable industry is a pokey one. It does not want to rewire Britain. It wants to cash in on an American-style explosion of pay-TV. But I am unhappy about the supervision of cable content. If cable is not to be an electronic newsagent, there is no point in encouraging it. Obscenity and libel can be discouraged, as they are in print, by the law of the land. After all, in America the most offensive programmes on cable television are not films or pay-TV, but the public-access channels. "Ugly George's Hour of Sex and Violence" is protected by the First Amendment to the Constitution − a guaranteed freedom of the press which does not exist in Britain.

So, half-hearted deregulation is what we are going to get here. Will it be the right half? Maybe not. Should what emerges be called deregulation? It might be better to paraphrase Charles Haughey's appraisal of Ireland's grudging legalisation on contraception: "a British solution to a British problem".

In the long run, the experience of television, as we have enjoyed it from the 1950s to the 1980s, will disappear. The whole family sitting around a television set is gone already. There are more and more sets. People have recorders to make their own schedules. My 12-year-old son, when he comes home from school, watches an X film taped from the night before instead of Blue Peter.

The fragmentation of the audience is inevitable, but it will be a slow process, and I am glad.

THE POLITICS OF INFORMATION POWER
STUART HOOD

There is a famous formula invented by one of the founding fathers of media studies which states that 'a convenient way to describe an act of communication is to answer the following question: Who Says What in Which Channel to Whom With What Effect?' It is a formula which its inventor, Lasswell, applied within the limits of a funtionalist analysis of the media – one which limited itself to describing their function within society without questioning their relationship to social structures, to economics and to power. It was, I think, Raymond Williams who pointed out that an essential question is missing from the list: namely – To What Purpose? I should like to go further and add: For Whose Benefit? But the formula, in either its original or its revised form, is worth applying to information technology because the question it poses can easily be overlooked in a rush of utopian fervour and the assumption that we are about to witness the breaking of the restraints imposed on communication, and their freeing from the forces of economic and political power.

It is worth recalling that the rockets used to put communications satellites into orbit are the linear descendants of the V2s which Werner von Braun invented to bombard London before he was taken over by NASA and his skills harnessed to the military and political requirements of the USA.

The development of rockets and the satellites they put into orbit have certainly as much to do with the requirements of the military-industrial complexes of the super-powers, and their global strategic aims. As a result we are spied on, monitored, threatened by satellites of immense sophistication; space is full of hardware which no doubt includes anti-satellite satellites (for who can doubt that the point could easily come where one of the superpowers decided to 'take out' the other's spy satellites?) More than two thirds of all satellites in orbit are military ones.

Communications are a by-product of military ends in much the same way as the non-stick frying-pan is said to be one of the by-products of putting astronauts on the moon. Which is not to say that there are not satellite systems in use serving the peaceful purposes of the political systems of the capitalist and the non-capitalist world – whether, like the Soviet Molnia and Ecran, Canada's Anik or the Indonesian satellite they are employed to guarantee communications over large areas of the globe, or like the USA's RCA satellite they are used for normal commercial purposes. Satellites carry immense quantities of different kinds of communication on a routine basis — so much so that the fact that moving pictures in a television newscast come on to our screens by way of a satellite transmission is no longer sufficiently remarkable to merit mention.

But Lasswell's question about who is saying what to whom is still worth asking. The answer is that in the case of television the messages are subject to the same processes of editorial adjustment on the part of those involved as all the other material that reaches our screens, which is carefully filtered at both a conscious and an unconscious level. The information we receive is mediated by the editorial assumptions of the broadcasting institutions and the international news agencies, who can afford to use the facilities afforded by satellite communications. A number of the ground stations which transmit to the information agencies of the West are in countries which for historical reasons — colonialism and neo-colonialism — continue to be exploited not only economically but in terms of communications. As the MacBride Report prepared for UNESCO points out, what such countries need is on the one hand access to communications systems so as to be able to make statements about their societies which are not slated towards the needs of the media in the advanced countries, and on the other the possibilities for developing not high-grade communications, but cheap and efficient local communication: video and print as a part of the immense task of education which will have to accompany the political and economical development of such countries.

If we look at the prospects for Europe we have to examine the prospects of the early introduction of DBS – direct broadcasting by satellites. Here once again the question of who is saying what and for what purpose is relevant. The BBC will very soon have access to two channels on a satellite beamed to the United Kingdon. In their case, we can take for granted who is making the statements and what is being said – the programmes and news radiated by satellite will be made within the constraints to which the BBC bows as part of its unwritten pact with the parliamentary consensus or (as in times of crisis like the Falklands War) with the government of the day. But the purpose is a financial one. What has been suggested by BBC spokesmen is that in order to have access to the satellite signal, viewers will require to pay a fee over and above the licence fee we now pay for the right to own and operate a television set. The BBC will in fact be introducing two-tier television – one service for the ordinary viewer and another for those who can afford it. It is a pattern already well established in the United States where Home Box Office provides 'better' programmes for viewers who are pre-pared to pay a considerable subscription to have access to the satellite signal.

The adoption of the two-tier system is therefore on the one hand a way to supplement the BBC's licence revenue; but the licence fee is itself more that a mere question of cash. It is also a political matter. The Corporation has found itself in recent years in financial straits because of inflation; this in turn has meant that it has had to go to Government to ask for increases in the licence fee. But the licence fee is notoriously a finely-tuned control system whose work-ings can be deduced from the way in which governments of what-ever hue have in recent years tended to grant the BBC a slightly lower rise than it has asked for or required. It was *The Guardian* that commented, when the last rise was being negotiated, that the BBC's decision to screen an interview with the Irish Republican groups which claimed to have caused the death of Airey Neve would jeopardise its chances of getting what it wanted.

A favourable interpretation of the BBC's decision to go into DBS and charge an additional fee would be that it sees in DBS a means of prising itself loose from strict government financial and therefore political control. The rightward movement of BBC management makes it seem optimistic to expect such independence of mind, and the motives are more likely to be purely commercial. On the other hand, the concept of two-tier television is an aban-donment of one of the fundamental and most positive elements in the Reithian philosophy of broadcasting: that is, the belief that it is the BBC's duty as a public service organisation to provide a signal to

viewers and listeners in all parts of the United Kingdon — a duty
which the IBA does not acknowledge as is evident from an examination of its coverage maps of the ITV transmitters; for the IBA
covers with its signals only those areas of the country where there
are sufficient viewers to be of interest to advertisers. Looked at
from this point of view, there are areas of the maps of Scotland and
Wales which remind one, in their blankness, of maps of Africa or
Australia before the days of the great explorers.

The question of commercial television's coverage of the United
Kingdom leads one logically to look at the probable aims of the
television consortia which are poised to move into DBS — consortia
which will be based in the UK, or more likely in Luxemburg, and
which will no doubt be funded and controlled by a mixture of
indigenous and international capital. In this case the purpose of the
broadcasts is obvious: to make profits for the business interests
involved. Whoever may be the glamorous speakerines chosen to
present the programmes and to charm the viewer into watching
them — one pilot programme had no less than three young women
to seal the programmes on the basis of sex appeal — the voice will be
the voice of the forces who put up the money. Their criteria — if the
forces of the market are allowed to have unrestricted play — are
those of the cost per thousand (the cost to the advertisers of each
thousand viewers 'delivered' to them by the bait of the programmes). The evidence of past performance shows that uncontrolled commercial broadcasting will follow the dictates of the profit
motive and abandon any programme addressed to a minority (unless it is very rich), or to sizeable majorities which do not happen to
include in their number people who have the spending power to buy
the products displayed on the screen.

This raises the question of control. If the example of commercial
television in Britain is anything to go by, there are ways of miti-
gating the purely greedy motives of the broadcasters and advertisers. Some of these have been devised by the IBA, which is — as
we know — by no means a perfect body in terms of its constitution
and record, but has at least the virtue of removing some areas of
television from the uncontrolled play of commercialism. What
looks out at us from the screen is still the face of capitalism, but not
— in consensus terms — its 'unacceptable' face.

It is when the question of control is raised that major problems
begin to present themselves both for the conservative forces which
wish to advance the new information technology for reasons of
profit, and to their radical critics who wish to see it used for more
enlightened social ends. Let us take the distribution of television
signals by cable as an example. Cable distribution is important as an

adjunct to satellite television, as a means to convey the signals to a maximum number of households. But cables are not needed if viewers can have their individual dish antennae to receive DBS signals. They are only needed if there will be centralised receiver antennae, from which the signals are then distributed by cable through a particular district or community.

The present government has decreed that this autumn decisions have to be made for the building of what is rather grandiosely called a national cable network − grandiosely, because the network will in fact be confined to the main conurbations, and remote communities(not to mention the countryside in general) will not be covered for obvious reasons of cost and profitability. It is notable that the government report that advocates the construction of this network at no point discussed the social need for it, nor is the scheme considered in any framework of relative priorities; and there are a great many of those, from the railways to preschool education, to better pay for hospital workers, which some people might think come higher up the list. It is significant too that the committee considering the question consisted of business interests, including a representative of Rediffusion, one of the main cable distributors; Rediffusion's history in communications − whether in broadcast television or in community cable television − shows that it has always believed that communications can be run and managed on the same lines as a chain of launderettes, or the British Electric Company of which it is a subsidiary.

The reasons for the Tory Government's determination to press on with a cable network are not far to seek. It is a further example of its determination to give private capital an opportunity to take profits out of what should (if at all) be a public communications system. In this sense it is part of the programme which aims to dismantle parts of the Post Office, or North Sea Gas. In this context the fact that one of the big cable companies is a contributor to Conservative party funds is not irrelevant.

Where the government (if it is still in power) − or indeed any government that replaces it − will run up against contradictions, is that a cable system capable of carrying a multiplicity of signals − a multiplicity made possible by the capabilities of fibre optic cables − once thrown open to the working of commercial interests, will be extraordinarily difficult to control. If the video cassette market is anything to go by, we can expect that programmes will include a large proportion (up to 40 per cent) of sado-masochism and soft porn. A multiplicity of signals makes for what is called a 'leaky' system, in the sense that the telephone system is leaky − too vast for control, except by a statistically limited, but still large, number of tapped lines. The fact is that, porn and sado-masochism apart, we are not living in an era when governments are likely to be anxious to encourage communications which are leaky to any great extent – liable, that is to say, to carry communications which challenge the views of the parliamentary consensus, that give a radical voice to minorities, to women, to gay people, or to the large ethnic communities that live in our society. How long would a Brixton community cable service, which really expressed the views of the black community on police methods in that area, be allowed to express itself freely? It is therefore not surprising that a number of representations have been made – by the IBA, for instance – calling for a controlling authority or for some sort of licensing system. The danger from the point of view of the consensus is that the expansion of information technology can in certain areas potentially challenge those control systems which, with the support of all parties in parliament, have been applied to broadcasting in this country since its earliest days. These control systems were rationalised on the grounds that the portion of the radio frequency spectrum available for broadcasting is limited. This is true – although there are more intelligent ways of using the spectrum, large portions of which are allocated to the police and the military. But the argument from scarcity falls down in the face of modern technology. There will be attempts to re-introduce it, for the desire for control was essentially political in nature, and reflected the fear that were broadcasting to be uncontrolled, undesirable opinions might get abroad. Indeed at one time there was a suggestion that amateur broadcasters might receive a licence to transmit only if they produced credentials to show that they were of good character.

The dilemma for radical critics of a cable distribution system, with all its capabilities for a multiplicity of voices, would arise if access to cable distribution were made readily available, if community interests were guaranteed against interference from outside, if voices from outside the consensus were to be heard. The dilemma would pose itself in the form of the question: Should the National Front or other racist organisations be allowed to have access on the same basis as others? Or the question: Should the potential of the new technology be used to disseminate representations of women which exploit them and invite the males in the audience to consider them as the objects for sexual abuse and sexual violence? The liberal answer is Yes. The radical answer to both is No. What has to be confronted here is the fundamental question of censorship, which is linked to the equally fundamental question of power or control; who says what through which channel. These are questions which radical critics of the present system shy away from but which will have to be confronted and answered theoretically and, hopefully, practically. For what it is worth, my own view is that no society is conceivable which does not set limits of one type or another to what may be said or discussed beyond a certain point in it at any historical conjuncture. Absolute freedom is not something which we can hope to experience or obtain; the best we may expect is that, within the limits of a given social system, the boundaries of freedom are kept as wide as possible and that they are vigilangly defended.

Power, then, in the form of control, is a fundamental problem. It applies to all forms of the new technology, whether it is satellites, cable systems, or videotext. Power stems from ownership and control, and from ownership and control stems editorial policy. Thus videotexts are not some neutral means of disseminating information. The crucial questions − to which few people know the answer − are who is formulating the information that appears on the screen; who decides who should be included in the pages of the videotext; on what ideological and political basis are the judgements involved in the editorial process based; why are certain terms used rather than others? It is one of the important functions of the media in society to suggest what certain individuals or groups within that society should be called: dissidents, trouble-makers, disruptive elements, enemies of the state, etc. Even if we do not know who is responsible for the material on our screens, we can be certain of one thing: that the information is not in some antiseptic way neutral.

Closely allied to the dissemination of information by videotexts is the use of video to interrogate viewers, either on programmes or on issues of wider importance: local political issues, for instance, or even matters of more general interest in the social and political field. Some futurologists contemplate with satisfaction and excitement a vision of the television audience sitting at home and using feed-back mechanisms to express their views: instant referenda. This is sometimes hailed as a triumph for democracy. What it is, in fact, is the application of the process of privatisation to the political process. Viewers in these circumstances would normally make their political and social judgements on the basis of the views presented to them by the media. Thus a feedback loop would be formed which is Orwellian in its symmetry. By this means the process of political decision-making by the members of our society would be removed from the area of debate and discussion − the shop floor, the union meeting, the political demonstration − and located safely in the cellular family. The criticism of this prophecy, with its suppression of participation, is the same as that which informs trade union opposition to the present government's desire to impose postal

AND THIS PROGRAM WILL
PLAY OFFICE POLITICS.

ballots on the unions; far from encouraging democracy it would be a move towards control and the stifling of debate.

There remains one area of information technology which vividly illustrates the problems of control; it is the area of computers. Computers are marvellous and probably now indispensable instruments for administration, for research, for medicine, for industrial processes; they are also instruments of power, whether used by multinationals to exchange information on the basis of which they switch their investments from one labour market to another in search of cheap labour, or whether used by the police and the military as instruments of control and repression. It is a characteristic of government to collect information about their citizens which those citizens are barred from inspecting or controlling. None of us in this room know what information is contained on what computers, who has access to that information or how accurate it is. There is evidence that a good deal of the information is in some cases inaccurate, based on rumour, gossip and misinformation. We do not know which computers link with which and how much information is transferred from perfectly legitimate sources – the computers of the National Health Service, for instance, to those of Special Branch and the security services. It is said that Northern Ireland has one of the most highly developed security systems in the West. The Federal German Republic has another. Hans Magnus Enzensberger has said that the image of the policeman as a tough with a rubber baton has largely been replaced by that of a computer programmer with a degree who can retrieve information about a very large number of the citizens of the Republic on the basis of information culled from a multitude of sources – including dentists, doctors, landlords, car salesmen, or fingerprints. Not everyone is as unfortunate as the woman in Hamburg whose flat was invaded and she herself stripped and searched because she had fingerprints which approximated to those of a wanted terrorist. The computer had got it wrong. When she enquired what she could do as a safeguard against a repetition of the incident, she was told: "You could always cut them off."

Technology is not neutral. It does not develop according to the laws of some technological determinism, breeding clinically according to some inner logic of development. It grows and flourishes in response to social, economic and political requirements. The computerised control of society is not immanent in the binary system which lies at the heart of all computers. It arises from the political needs of particular societies, and of those who run them. Let me close with a quotation from the MacBride Report:

"The technological explosion in communications has both great potential and great danger. The outcome depends on crucial decisions and on where and by whom they are taken. Thus it is a priority to organise the decision-making process in a participatory manner on the basis of a full awareness of the social impact of different alternatives".

Such a policy would be one element in an interesting political programme. Which party do you think will include it in its electoral manifesto?

THERE'S BETTER WAYS OF GETTING IN THE SUNDAY PAPERS THAN HAVING A RECORD ON THE POLICE COMPUTER, SON.

Brief biographies

Alan Benjamin: is the Communication Director of The CAP Group Ltd., one of Britain's leading information systems companies. He is Chairman of the British Computer Society Specialist Group for Developing Countries and is a member of the UK Council for Computing Development. His previous experience included the founding of software house SPL International and was the first Director General of the Computer Services Association.

Mike Cooley: was a member of the Lucas Aerospace Combine Shop Stewards Committee involved in drawing up the Lucas workers' alternative plan. He is now working for the Economic Policy Group of the Greater London Coucil and is developing alternative eonomic policies and plans for London.

Rita Cruise O'Brien: is a Fellow at the Institute of Development Studies. She has published articles and books on African development and international mass media issues in the 1970's. She has also edited a book close to the subject of the contribution in this volume, *Information, Economics and Power: The North-South Dimension,* forthcoming 1983, and is currently working on a more general project, *The Politics of the Information Age.*

Dr. John Dawson: Head of the Professional, Scientific and International Affairs Division at the British Medical Association. Qualified in medicine 1970, and trained in anaesthetics and general practice. Worked as medical officer to the British Antarctic Survey, wintering at Halley Bay, before joining the BMA.

David Fairbairn: was appointed Director of the National Computing Centre in March 1980. He previously held appointments with EMI Medical Ltd, International Computers Ltd and the Guinness Company. He is Vice-President of the Institute of Data Processing Management and a Fellow of the British Computer Society.

Jonothan Gershuny: Senior Fellow of Science Policy Research Unit University of Sussex. Author of *After Industrial Society?,* Macmillan 1978; *Social Innovation and the Division of Labour,* Oxford University Press, forthcoming, and numerous other articles and monographs. Current research on relationship between lifestyles and economic structures.

Patricia Hewitt: General Secretary, National Council for Civil Liberties since 1974. Formerly women's rights officer, NCCL; public relations officer, Age concern. Author, *The Abuse of Power: Civil Liberties in the United Kingdom; Privacy : The Information-Gatherers;* and numerous articles and pamplets. Prospective Labour Parliamentary Candidate, Leicester East, since 1981.

Stuart Hood: Studied Eng Lit at Edinburgh University. Taught briefly. Six years in the army. Joined BBC on demobilisation and was at various times head of the General Overseas Service (World Service), Editor Television News and Controller of Programmes, BBC TV. Short disastrous period with commercial television. Freelance documentary film-maker, script-writer for BBC and ITV. Author of three novels, an autobiography and books on the media. Was Professor of Film and TV at Royal College of Art. Lecturer in media studies and theory of film.

John Howkins: is a writer on the media and communications, and is editor of *Intermedia,* the journal of the International Institute of Communications. His publications this year include *Mass Communications in China* (Longman) and *New Technologies, New Policies* (British Film Institute), a briefing paper for the BFI's Working Party on New Technologies. He is Programme Director of The Economist/IIC conference on cable television to be held in London in February 1983. He is chairman of the London International Film School.

Clive Jenkins: is the General Secretary of ASTMS – a member of the TUC General Council, Chairman of the TUC Education Committee, a trustee of the National Heritage Memorial Fund, a former Board Member of the National Research Development Corporation and the British National Oil Corporation. He co-authored The Collapse of Work and the Leisure Shock.

Brenda Maddox: author and home affairs editor of The Economist, is an internationally recognised writer on communication policy. Her book, "Beyond Babel: New Directions in Communication," published by Andre Deutsch, 1972, is a prescient analasis of the impact of cable television and satellite on the conventional structures of broadcasting and telecommunications.

Christopher Price MP: was born in Leeds in 1932, was a schoolteacher in Southampton and Sheffield, before being elected to Parliament in 1966. He is now Chairman of the House of Commons Select Committee on Education, Science and the Arts which has produced reports on higher education, the Arts, and the storage and retrieval of information in the Library Service.

Dr. Juan Rada: is a member of the Faculty of the International Management Institute, Geneva; a consultant to the United Nations Centre for Transnational Corporations, to the International Labour office, the Inter-Governmental Bureau of Informatics and the United Nations Industrial Development Organisation; and he has recently become a member of the Club of Rome. Dr. Rada attended the Catholic University of Chile and holds a PHD from the University of London.

Paul Sieghart: is the Chairman of the Executive Committee of Justice, the British Section of the International Commission of Jurists. He drafted the Right of Privacy Bill 1970, and the Rehabilitation of Offenders Act 1974. In 1975, he helped Roy Jenkins to write that year's Home Office White Paper on 'Computers and Privacy', and subsequently served as a member of the government's Committee on Data Protection (the Lindop Committee). He is the author of *Privacy and Computers* (1976), and *The International Law of Human Rights* (1982). For several years, he was a director of a leading computer software house.

Ralph Shuffrey: is a Deputy Under Secretary of State at the Home Office. After service in the Army he read Classics at Balliol College, Oxford and joined the Home Office in 1951. He has served in a variety of Home Office Departments including civil defence, police, crime, immigration and fire and a spell as Private Secretary to Mr Roy Jenkins. Latterly he has been in charge of the General Department and he now deals with the staffing and organisation of the Home Office and has a particular responsibility for privacy and data protection.

Shirley Williams: was born in 1930. She was educated in the United States and Britain, reading PPE at Somerville, Oxford. In 1964 she was elected to the House of Commons as Labour member for Hitchin and in 1967 she became Minister of State at the Department of Education and Science. She held numerous posts both in and out of government until 1979. She is co-founder and now President of the Social Democratic Party and was elected as MP for Crosby in 1982.

Comedia Publishing Group

No. 13   MICROCHIPS WITH EVERYTHING –
The consequences of information technology
edited by Paul Sieghart   paperback £3.50 hardback £9.50

No. 12   THE WORLD WIRED UP –
Unscrambling the new communications puzzle
by Brian Murphy   paperback £3.50 hardback £9.50

No. 11   WHAT'S THIS CHANNEL FOUR? An alternative report
edited by Simon Blanchard and David Morley
paperback £3.50 hardback £9.50

No. 10   IT AIN'T HALF RACIST, MUM – Fighting racism in the media
edited by Phil Cohen and Carl Gardner
paperback £2.50 hardback £7.50

No. 9   NUKESPEAK – The media and the bomb
edited by Crispin Aubrey   paperback £2.50 hardback £7.50

No. 8   NOT the BBC/IBA – The case for community radio
by Simon Partridge   paperback £1.95 hardback £5.00

No. 7   CHANGING THE WORD –
The printing industry in transition
by Alan Marshall   paperback £3.50 hardback £9.50

No. 6   THE REPUBLIC OF LETTERS –
Working class writing and local publishing
edited by David Morley and Ken Worpole
paperback £2.95 hardback £8.50

No. 5   NEWS LTD – Why you can't read all about it
by Brian Whitaker   paperback £3.25 hardback £9.50

No. 4   ROLLING YOUR OWN –
Women as printers, publishers and distributors
by Eileen Cadman, Gail Chester, Agnes Pivot
paperback £2.50 hardback £9.50

No. 3   THE OTHER SECRET SERVICE –
Press distribution and press censorship
by Liz Cooper, Charles Landry, Dave Berry
paperback only £0.80

No. 2   **WHERE IS THE OTHER NEWS –**
The news trade and the radical press
by Dave Berry, Liz Cooper, Charles Landry
paperback £1.75

No. 1   **HERE IS THE OTHER NEWS –**
Challenges to the local commercial press
by Crispin Aubrey, Charles Landry, Dave Morley
hardback £3.50